Switch It Up

A FRESH TAKE ON QUICK AND EASY
DIABETES-FRIENDLY RECIPES FOR A BALANCED LIFE

Corinne Trang

American Diabetes Association.

Director, Book Publishing, Abe Ogden; Managing Editor, Project Manager, Rebekah Renshaw; Acquisitions Editor, Victor Van Beuren; Production Manager, Melissa Sprott; Composition, Circle Graphics; Cover Design, Vis-à-Vis; Printer, Versa Press.

Printed in the United States of America
1 3 5 7 9 10 8 6 4 2

The suggestions and information contained in this publication are generally consistent with the *Standards of Medical Care in Diabetes* and other policies of the American Diabetes Association, but they do not represent the policy or position of the Association or any of its boards or committees. Reasonable steps have been taken to ensure the accuracy of the information presented. However, the American Diabetes Association cannot ensure the safety or efficacy of any product or service described in this publication. Individuals are advised to consult a physician or other appropriate health care professional before undertaking any diet or exercise program or taking any medication referred to in this publication. Professionals must use and apply their own professional judgment, experience, and training and should not rely solely on the information contained in this publication before prescribing any diet, exercise, or medication. The American Diabetes Association—its officers, directors, employees, volunteers, and members—assumes no responsibility or liability for personal or other injury, loss, or damage that may result from the suggestions or information in this publication.

♾ The paper in this publication meets the requirements of the ANSI Standard Z39.48-1992 (permanence of paper).

ADA titles may be purchased for business or promotional use or for special sales. To purchase more than 50 copies of this book at a discount, or for custom editions of this book with your logo, contact the American Diabetes Association at the address below or at booksales@diabetes.org.

American Diabetes Association

2451 Crystal Drive, Suite 900
Arlington, VA 22202

DOI: 10.2337/9781580405492

Library of Congress Cataloging-in-Publication Data
Names: Trang, Corinne, author.
Title: Switch It Up: A Fresh Take On Quick and Easy Diabetes-Friendly Recipes for A Balanced Life/Corinne Trang.
Other titles: Switch it up
Description: Alexandria : American Diabetes Association, [2017]
Identifiers: LCCN 2016013739 | ISBN 9781580405492 (paperback)
Subjects: LCSH: Diabetes—Diet therapy—Popular works | Diabetes—Nutritional
   aspects—Popular works. | BISAC: COOKING / Health & Healing / Diabetic &
   Sugar-Free. | COOKING / Health & Healing / Weight Control. | HEALTH &
   FITNESS / Weight Loss. | COOKING / Health & Healing / Heart. | LCGFT:
   Cookbooks.
Classification: LCC RC662 .T742 2016 | DDC 641.5/6314—dc23
LC record available at https://lccn.loc.gov/2016013739

For Colette

You are my inspiration.
May you always be healthy and happy.

ACKNOWLEDGMENTS

It is always a great opportunity to collaborate on projects with folks whose mission is to focus on wellbeing. Much like my *Asian Flavors Diabetes Cookbook*, which won the Nautilus Cookbook Award, this new book is intended for those living with diabetes and their family and friends with whom they share their table. May you focus on and find great satisfaction and pleasure in the foods you can have. Thank you to the millions living with this condition, for giving me the opportunity to create quick and easy recipes for maintaining a healthy and balanced lifestyle.

My work as a holistic health and nutrition counselor has always been fascinating, creating recipes for clients, each one living with challenges, oftentimes diabetes, but not limited to this condition. How to put my teachings down on paper to address a wider audience, has not always been easy because everyone is unique. This book isn't just for people with diabetes. It's also perfect for those diagnosed with pre-diabetes, heart disease, and other health conditions. Diet and exercise are the foundation to healthy living.

Switch It Up

Thank you to my agent and dear friend Beth Shepard of Beth Shepard Communications, LLC. She has been my rock and guiding light in numerous projects including this one. I am ever so grateful for our ongoing collaboration, and look forward to many more.

Thank you, Rebekah Renshaw, Managing Editor, who has seen this project through its multiple phases to the end. Thanks also to Katie Curran, Marketing Manager, as well as Circle Graphics, who created a beautiful user-friendly book.

Thank you to friends and family for putting up with my absences, which are always with great regret but clearly for a greater good.

Here's to a healthy you!

Corinne Trang

TABLE OF CONTENTS

SOUPS

WHOLE GRAINS & LEGUMES

EGGS, SEAFOOD, & MEAT

FRUIT, CHEESE, NUTS, & SEEDS

INTRODUCTION

Imagine food that can be made ahead of time for convenience, and then mixed and matched to create colorful, perfectly portioned meals that are both healthful and flavorful. **Switch It Up** lets you discover how the concept of compartmentalizing can help you prepare balanced meals for every day of the week.

You'll learn how to pair different flavors and textures while developing a palate for healthful food combinations. Healthy eating starts with understanding balance. For instance, in Asian cultures the majority of the meal is made up of vegetables, with much less animal or seafood protein than we are used to in the West. Anything with legs or fins is generally considered a flavor enhancer rather than the main course. A small amount goes a long way! Keeping that in mind, I have given you more vegetarian recipes than meat or seafood ones, to give you the chance to incorporate more vegetables into your meals, reducing fat significantly along the way.

Additionally, salt and sugar are kept to a minimum to allow you to taste food in its natural state, so that you may appreciate and understand it better before "fixing" it. Too often we season without even tasting, resulting in foods that are overly sweet or salty. We develop an addiction to these and eventually suffer for it, physically, mentally, and emotionally.

Furthermore, you can decide to enjoy the "Raw Kale and Roasted Sweet Potato Salad" (page 26) as a full meal or as a part of a meal, if you wanted to pair the salad with other foods. Lastly, desserts are largely absent; fresh fruit or a simple cup of hot tea or herbal infusion is encouraged at the end of the meal to aid digestion.

This book includes 50 simple, quick, and nutritious recipes that you can combine in any number of ways. Each recipe is made up of readily available ingredients to give you a one-stop-shopping option and save you time. You'll also notice that the recipes offer different flavor profiles inspired by cuisines from around the world. From here, I encourage you to visualize the content of this book as an actual dinner plate, noticing that it is about 70–75% vegetarian. Now start visualizing every meal this way and you're on your way to a healthier you.

Bon appétit!

Corinne Trang

SALADS & VEGETABLES

You can never have enough vegetables. Fiber is necessary for proper digestion and fiber comes from plant-based foods. The higher the fiber content of your meals, the healthier you will be. Here you'll find interesting salad combinations and sautéed, braised, or roasted vegetables to give you a variety of textures.

Some raw food is necessary to ensure your body gets plenty of nutrients. Once heated, some vegetables can lose some of their vitamins and minerals, though they retain plenty of flavor and fiber. A good mix at every meal is highly recommended. When creating your plate, consider choosing a salad and a cooked vegetable. Now you have at least two vegetable options for your meal.

Shaved Raw Brussels Sprout Salad with Blueberries and Parmesan

SERVES 8

SERVING 1 cup

PREP 35 minutes

COOK O minutes

PAIRING SUGGESTION
Rosemary-Sage Turkey Breast (page 90) and Brown Rice & Broccoli Salad with Nuts and Seeds (page 52)

INGREDIENTS
Juice of 1 lemon (about 1/4 cup)
1 teaspoon Dijon mustard
1/4 cup extra virgin olive oil
1/3 cup freshly grated Parmesan
1 pound Brussels sprouts, trimmed and paper-thinly sliced (about 6 cups)
1 1/2 cups fresh blueberries
Freshly ground black pepper to taste

Brussels sprouts are naturally sweet and are delicious raw. With fresh blueberries for color and a lemon-Parmesan dressing, they make for a delicious option that is sweet, sour, and salty. The spicy and bitter notes come from freshly cracked black pepper. This salad can keep a few days in the refrigerator. The longer they marinate in the tangy dressing, the softer the Brussels sprouts get.

In a large bowl, whisk together the lemon juice and mustard until well combined. Whisk in the oil until smooth, and stir in half the Parmesan. Add the Brussels sprouts and toss well to distribute the dressing. Let stand for 20 minutes and toss again. Add the blueberries, toss lightly, and transfer to a serving plate or a container. Scatter the remaining Parmesan on top and season with pepper.

EXCHANGES / CHOICES
1/2 Fruit
1 Vegetable
1 1/2 Fat

Calories	110
Calories from Fat	70
Total Fat	8.0 g
Saturated Fat	1.5 g
Trans Fat	0.0 g
Cholesterol	0 mg
Sodium	75 mg
Potassium	230 mg
Total Carbohydrate	9 g
Dietary Fiber	3 g
Sugars	4 g
Protein	3 g
Phosphorus	60 mg

Rosemary-Sage Turkey
Breast (page 90)

Brown Rice & Broccoli
Salad with Nuts and Seeds
(page 52)

Oak Leaf Lettuce and Pear Salad with Stilton

SERVES 8

SERVING 1 cup

PREP 20 minutes

COOK 0 minutes

PAIRING SUGGESTION

Pork Lettuce Wrap with Prune Relish (page 94) and Baby Bok Choy Stir-Fried with Ginger and Garlic (page 18)

INGREDIENTS

2 tablespoons red wine vinegar

1 teaspoon Dijon mustard

3 tablespoons extra virgin olive oil

Salt and pepper to taste

4 cups freshly torn lettuce of your choice

1 ripe green or red Anjou pear, cored and cut into wedges (or any fruit in season)

1 ounce Stilton or any blue cheese, crumbled

2 tablespoons raw or roasted, unsalted pecans

I love a good salad made with mature lettuce, rather than the ever so popular mesclun mix. Tender oak leaf lettuce (both red and green) is delicious against juicy Anjou pears, crunchy pecans, and creamy, salty Stilton. It's a great combination any time of the year, though take advantage of the seasons, for berries are also delicious in salads during the summer. If you like different textures and colors, add some frisée and radicchio to the mix!

1. In a small bowl, whisk together the vinegar and mustard until well combined. Whisk in the olive oil, salt, and pepper until smooth and thickened, and season with salt and pepper to taste.

2. In a large shallow salad bowl, scatter the lettuce leaves and top with pear and Stilton. Sprinkle with pecans and drizzle the dressing on top. Let stand for 15 minutes without tossing so as to keep the lettuce from wilting, and serve.

Mature lettuce is more flavorful and retains its texture much better than any baby green. Buy different heads of lettuce, separate the leaves, wash and spin thoroughly, and then store them in the refrigerator separately in 1- or 2-gallon sealable bags for up to one week. You can stick a paper towel in each bag to absorb any excess water. This way, they will stay crisp.

EXCHANGES / CHOICES
1/2 Fruit
1 1/2 Fat

Calories	90
Calories from Fat	65
Total Fat	7.0 g
Saturated Fat	1.5 g
Trans Fat	0.0 g
Cholesterol	5 mg
Sodium	70 mg
Potassium	85 mg
Total Carbohydrate	5 g
Dietary Fiber	1 g
Sugars	3 g
Protein	1 g
Phosphorus	30 mg

Pork Lettuce Wrap with
Prune Relish (page 94)

Baby Bok Choy
Stir-Fried with Ginger and
Garlic (page 18)

Fennel Salad with Blood Orange

SERVES 8

SERVING 1 cup

PREP 15 minutes

COOK 0 minutes

PAIRING SUGGESTION

Crab Cakes with Parsnip Purée (page 84) and Quinoa with Kale and Dried Cranberries (page 56)

INGREDIENTS

2 fennel bulbs, shaved or paper-thinly sliced (about 6 cups), some fronds reserved for garnish

4 blood oranges, peeled and sectioned, membranes removed, any juice squeezed and reserved

2 tablespoons extra virgin olive oil

Salt, to taste

Pepper, to taste

A classic Italian salad, this delicate and refreshing shaved fennel salad with blood orange is an unexpected combination of flavors and colors. Keep the delicious fennel fronds to garnish and add color to the dish.

In a medium bowl, toss the fennel and blood oranges. Squeeze the juice from the orange membrane over the salad. Drizzle with olive oil and season with salt and pepper. Garnish with fennel fronds and serve.

When sectioning citrus fruit, there is always juicy pulp left behind. Squeeze the membrane over a bowl to get all of the juice out and reserve it for making salad dressings.

EXCHANGES / CHOICES
1/2 Fruit
1 Vegetable
1 Fat

Calories	85
Calories from Fat	30
Total Fat	3.5 g
Saturated Fat	0.5 g
Trans Fat	0.0 g
Cholesterol	0 mg
Sodium	35 mg
Potassium	410 mg
Total Carbohydrate	14 g
Dietary Fiber	4 g
Sugars	9 g
Protein	2 g
Phosphorus	45 mg

Crab Cakes with Parsnip
Purée (page 84)

Quinoa with Kale and
Dried Cranberries (page 56)

Raw Zucchini Salad with Prunes

SERVES 8

SERVING 1 cup

PREP 15 minutes

COOK 0 minutes

PAIRING SUGGESTION

Miso Soup with Crispy Tofu and Refreshing Cucumber (page 48) and Broiled Miso Salmon (page 80)

INGREDIENTS

1 tablespoon light soy sauce

1/2 teaspoon sriracha hot chili sauce

2 tablespoons rice vinegar

1 tablespoon grapeseed oil

1 teaspoon dark sesame oil

1 teaspoon freshly grated ginger

4 small-medium zucchini, julienned

8 dried pitted prunes, paper-thinly sliced

Zucchini is delicious raw, retaining its crunchy texture, not to mention vitamins. Here it is julienned, tossed with sweet prunes, and seasoned with a ginger-soy dressing. Be sure to select zucchini that are firm to the touch.

In a bowl, whisk together the soy sauce, sriracha, rice vinegar, grapeseed and sesame oils, and ginger. Toss in the zucchini and prunes.

EXCHANGES / CHOICES
1/2 Carbohydrate
1/2 Fat

Calories	60
Calories from Fat	20
Total Fat	2.5 g
Saturated Fat	0.3 g
Trans Fat	0.0 g
Cholesterol	0 mg
Sodium	85 mg
Potassium	325 mg
Total Carbohydrate	9 g
Dietary Fiber	2 g
Sugars	5 g
Protein	2 g
Phosphorus	45 mg

Miso Soup with Crispy Tofu
and Refreshing Cucumber
(page 48)

Broiled Miso Salmon
(page 80)

Ratatouille

SERVES 8

SERVING cup

PREP 20 minutes

COOK 1 hour

PAIRING SUGGESTION

Shaved Raw Brussels Sprout
Salad with Blueberries and
Parmesan (page 2) and Curry-
Spiced Chicken Breasts (page 88)

INGREDIENTS

1/4 cup olive oil

4 large garlic cloves, crushed,
    peeled, and chopped

1 medium onion, peeled and
    chopped

1 jalapeño, halved, seeded, and
    chopped (optional)

2 yellow bell peppers, cut into
    1-inch pieces

1 medium globe eggplant, cut
    into 1-inch pieces

2 small-medium zucchini, cut
    into 1-inch rounds

4 ripe plum tomatoes, cut into
    1-inch pieces

3 sprigs fresh thyme

12 large fresh basil leaves

1/2 cup water

Salt and pepper to taste

Ratatouille is a southern French specialty of braised zucchini, eggplant, peppers, and tomatoes. In its simplest form, it includes some fresh thyme and is seasoned with salt and pepper. Occasionally, it's fun to add a jalapeño to spice up your meal. This is the basis for another French dish called "Pipérade," which is leftover ratatouille with eggs, or Baked Eggs with Ratatouille and Parmesan (page 72).

In a large heavy-bottom pot over medium heat, add the oil and sauté the garlic until fragrant, about 30 seconds. Add the onion and jalapeño (if desired), and cook, stirring occasionally, until golden and caramelized, about 15 minutes. Add the bell peppers, eggplant, zucchini, tomatoes, thyme, basil, and 1/2 cup water. Turn the heat down to low and simmer, partially covered, until the vegetables are soft, 30–45 minutes. Season with salt and pepper.

While cooking, the vegetables will give up a lot of their natural juices. Remove the cover to allow some to evaporate. You can have as much juice or as little as you wish. There is no rule and it's entirely up to you. Drizzling the juice over rice can be delicious too.

3 Vegetable
1 Fat

Calories	115
Calories from Fat	65
Total Fat	7.0 g
Saturated Fat	1.0 g
Trans Fat	0.0 g
Cholesterol	0 mg
Sodium	10 mg
Potassium	400 mg
Total Carbohydrate	13 g
Dietary Fiber	3 g
Sugars	5 g
Protein	2 g
Phosphorus	55 mg

Shaved Raw Brussels Sprout Salad with Blueberries and Parmesan (page 2)

Curry-Spiced Chicken Breasts (page 88)

Eggplant, Tomato, and Mozzarella Napoleon

SERVES 8

SERVING 1 Napoleon

PREP 15 minutes

COOK 30 minutes

PAIRING SUGGESTION
Fennel Salad with Blood Orange
(page 6)

INGREDIENTS

5 tablespoons olive oil, divided
    use

16 large cloves garlic

Salt and pepper to taste

1 purple eggplant, sliced into
    1/4-inch-thick rounds

6 medium tomatoes, sliced into
    1/2-inch-thick rounds

16 fresh basil leaves

4 ounces part-skim mozzarella,
    sliced into 8 equal rounds

A Napoleon doesn't always have to be a sweet pastry. In fact, it's really good when made with vegetables stacked and topped with mozzarella and baked in the oven until golden. This dish is a beautiful presentation full of colors, flavors, and textures that complement one another. It is a great lunch or dinner. Enjoy with a refreshing tossed salad on the side.

1 Set broiler on "High" and preheat for 20 minutes.

2 In the meantime, working in batches, in a large nonstick skillet over medium heat, add 1 tablespoon oil and sauté the garlic cloves until golden. Remove from skillet and reserve. Add 2 tablespoons oil, and seasoning with salt and pepper as you go, pan-crisp half the eggplant until tender yet slightly firm, about 8 minutes total, flipping once. Using the remaining oil (a little at a time), repeat with the remaining eggplant, and then do the same with the tomatoes, cooking them until golden, about 4 minutes, flipping once.

3 To make the Napoleons, stack the vegetables in this order, in individual baking dishes: 1 slice each eggplant, tomato, basil leaf, repeat once more, and top with 1 slice mozzarella and some caramelized garlic cloves. Place in the oven and broil until the cheese has melted, about 5 minutes. Serve hot.

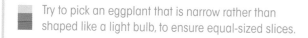

Try to pick an eggplant that is narrow rather than shaped like a light bulb, to ensure equal-sized slices.

While these are meant to be single-portion Napoleons, if you do not have enough individual dishes, you can always layer the vegetables in a large baking dish, following the recipe, and when baked, simply slice into multiple portions, much as you would lasagna.

EXCHANGES / CHOICES
3 Vegetable
1 Fat

Calories	120
Calories from Fat	55
Total Fat	6.0 g
Saturated Fat	2.0 g
Trans Fat	0.0 g
Cholesterol	10 mg
Sodium	95 mg
Potassium	400 mg
Total Carbohydrate	13 g
Dietary Fiber	3 g
Sugars	5 g
Protein	6 g
Phosphorus	115 mg

Fennel Salad with Blood
Orange (page 6)

Roasted Brussels Sprouts and Butternut Squash

SERVES 8

SERVING 1 cup

PREP 15 minutes

COOK 20 minutes

PAIRING SUGGESTION

Oak Leaf Lettuce and Pear Salad with Stilton (page 4) and Curry-Spiced Chicken Breasts (page 88)

INGREDIENTS

1 pound Brussels sprouts, trimmed, large ones halved

1/2 medium butternut squash, peeled, seeded, and cut into bite-size pieces (about 4 cups)

Salt and pepper to taste

2 tablespoons olive oil

1/2 teaspoon curry powder (optional, if not using bacon)

1/4 cup chopped bacon (optional, if not using curry)

Brussels sprouts are underrated. The trick to cooking Brussels sprouts is to cook them until tender and the natural sugars caramelize. Butternut squash is also one of my favorite autumn vegetables. Not only are the deep green of the Brussels sprouts and bright orange color of the butternut beautiful, but their combined textures create something unexpected, simple, and yet so satisfying.

1 Preheat the oven to 400°F for 20 minutes.

2 In a mixing bowl, add the Brussels sprouts and butternut squash. Drizzle with oil and toss well. Scatter in a roasting pan and cook in the oven until tender on the inside and crispy golden on the outside, about 20 minutes.

You can really have fun with this dish, by seasoning the vegetables lightly with curry powder before roasting or adding a strip of chopped bacon, trimming the fat first, for a different flavor and heartier dish.

EXCHANGES / CHOICES

1/2 Starch
1 Vegetable
1/2 Fat

Calories	70
Calories from Fat	30
Total Fat	3.5 g
Saturated Fat	0.5 g
Trans Fat	0.0 g
Cholesterol	0 mg
Sodium	15 mg
Potassium	315 mg
Total Carbohydrate	9 g
Dietary Fiber	3 g
Sugars	2 g
Protein	2 g
Phosphorus	45 mg

Oak Leaf Lettuce and Pear
Salad with Stilton (page 4)

Curry-Spiced Chicken
Breasts (page 88)

Roasted Root Vegetables with Garlic

SERVES 8

SERVING 1 cup

PREP 15 minutes

COOK 30 minutes

PAIRING SUGGESTION
Oak Leaf Lettuce and Pear Salad with Stilton (page 4)

INGREDIENTS

3 medium carrots, peeled and cut into 1/2-inch-thick rounds

2 medium red beets, cut into bite-size cubes (roughly 3/4 inch)

2 medium purple potatoes, cut into bite-size cubes (roughly 3/4 inch)

2 medium white potatoes, cut into bite-size cubes (roughly 3/4 inch)

1 head garlic, cloves separated, crushed lightly, and skins left on

3 tablespoons olive oil

Salt and pepper to taste

Fresh thyme

Autumn is a wonderful time for root vegetables. They make for a colorful, not to mention delicious center-piece at the table during the holidays. Feel free to experiment with your favorite root vegetables. I like a variety of colors and flavors. Sometimes, I just like using heirloom carrots of various colors from the typical orange to yellow, red, and purple ones as well. Roasted caramelized garlic cloves add another dimension to this dish as well. A simple wholesome meal doesn't require much more than that; the root vegetables are so filling that animal protein isn't required to complete the meal. Instead, go light with a touch of cheese with leafy greens either before or after.

1 Preheat the oven to 400°F for 20 minutes.

2 Arrange the carrots, beets, potatoes, and garlic cloves on one or two roasting pans or baking sheets. Drizzle with olive oil and season with salt and pepper. Roast until tender and golden, about 30 minutes. Peel garlic cloves and serve sprinkled with fresh thyme.

Not every oven is the same. Temperatures differ from one brand to the next, and there is a huge difference in temperature between a gas and electric oven. Gas ranges need to be calibrated regularly, while electric ones do not. Check your vegetables every once in a while to ensure correct doneness!

EXCHANGES / CHOICES
1 Starch
1 Vegetable
1 Fat

Calories	140	
Calories from Fat	45	
Total Fat	5.0	g
Saturated Fat	0.7	g
Trans Fat	0.0	g
Cholesterol	0	mg
Sodium	35	mg
Potassium	565	mg
Total Carbohydrate	22	g
Dietary Fiber	3	g
Sugars	3	g
Protein	3	g
Phosphorus	75	mg

Oak Leaf Lettuce and Pear
Salad with Stilton (page 4)

Baby Bok Choy Stir-Fried with Ginger and Garlic

SERVES 8

SERVING 1 cup

PREP 10 minutes

COOK 5 minutes

PAIRING SUGGESTION
Ginger Lobster Salad (page 86)
and Apple Cranberry Pecan Crisp
(page 100)

INGREDIENTS

1 1/2 tablespoons grapeseed oil

1 large garlic clove, crushed, peeled, and chopped or sliced

1 ounce ginger (about 1-inch piece), peeled and finely julienned or minced

1/2 pound leafy greens such as bok choy, quartered lengthwise

1 tablespoon light soy sauce

1 teaspoon dark sesame oil

Pepper to taste

Stir-frying is an Asian cooking technique that is easy to master. The trick is to not overload the skillet or wok and to keep the ingredients moving by continuously tossing them over high heat, which allows any accumulation of water to evaporate instantly. Stir-frying is a high-heat cooking technique; for this reason, grapeseed or vegetable oil, rather than olive oil, is recommended.

Place your wok or stainless steel skillet over high heat. Add the grapeseed oil and stir-fry the garlic and ginger until fragrant and light golden, about 30 seconds. Add the leafy greens, season with soy sauce, and continue to stir-fry until just wilted, 1–2 minutes, depending on the vegetable. (Chunky vegetables like broccoli and bell peppers take 2–3 minutes longer). Toss in the sesame oil, season with pepper, and transfer to a serving plate.

Have you ever wondered what it takes to flavor a traditional carbon steel wok to ensure a delicious stir-fry every time? Add a little oil and stir-fry garlic and ginger, and if the recipe calls for it, scallion. Create your stir-fry. As soon as you remove the cooked food, sprinkle the wok with kosher salt and let stand while you eat. This will absorb any cooking juices and or burnt bits. Take a paper towel and rub the salt into the wok's surface in a circular motion. Rinse with hot water, dry over high heat, let cool, and then rub a very thin layer of oil on top and store.

Each leafy green cooks differently. Some will require just a few seconds to cook, like spinach, Swiss chard, or watercress. Tougher greens such as cabbage, kale, or broccoli, will require more time. Know your vegetables and look for a just-wilted, yet somewhat firm consistency.

EXCHANGES / CHOICES
1 Fat

Calories	35
Calories from Fat	25
Total Fat	3.0 g
Saturated Fat	0.3 g
Trans Fat	0.0 g
Cholesterol	0 mg
Sodium	90 mg
Potassium	90 mg
Total Carbohydrate	2 g
Dietary Fiber	0 g
Sugars	0 g
Protein	1 g
Phosphorus	15 mg

Ginger Lobster Salad (page 86)

Apple Cranberry Pecan Crisp (page 100)

Artichoke Hearts with Vinaigrette

SERVES 8

SERVING 2 pieces

PREP 20 minutes

COOK 10 minutes

PAIRING SUGGESTION

Pan-Seared Pork Tenderloin with Sautéed Apples (page 92) and Shaved Raw Brussels Sprout Salad with Blueberries and Parmesan (page 2)

INGREDIENTS

1/4 cup olive oil

16 small (not "baby") globe artichokes, stems and leaves removed, chokes scraped clean

2 teaspoons Dijon mustard

3 tablespoons white or red wine vinegar

1/3 cup olive oil

2 scallions, trimmed and thinly sliced

Salt and pepper to taste

In Italy, artichokes are generally stuffed with bread-crumbs, cheese, and herbs. In the U.S., they are served with mayonnaise on the side for dipping. In France, they are often served plain, boiled, or steamed with a light tangy vinaigrette spiced with Dijon mustard. At least that's how my grandmother used to serve them and that's how I love them. Simple and healthy, the vinaigrette celebrates the natural flavor and lightness of this beautiful thistle bud! And while it takes patience to scrape through every single petal, the hearts are what most people love. The hearts, or chokes, however, are delicious pan-crisped in a bit of olive oil and water until tender on the inside and golden on the outside. Drizzled with the vinaigrette and topped with scallions, they make for a great starter.

1 In a large pan, over medium heat, add the oil with 1/4 cup water. Add the chokes and cook until the water evaporates and the chokes start crisping, flipping them occasionally, about 8 minutes.

2 Meanwhile in a bowl, whisk together the mustard with vinegar until well combined. Whisk in the olive oil until smooth and the sauce slightly thickened. Season with salt and pepper, drizzle lightly over each serving, and garnish with scallion.

 Season lightly with salt as Dijon mustard is already salty. Depending on the brand, salting may not be necessary at all.

 Chokes can be scraped clean with the edge of a teaspoon.

EXCHANGES / CHOICES
1 Vegetable
2 Fat

Calories	120
Calories from Fat	100
Total Fat	11.0 g
Saturated Fat	1.5 g
Trans Fat	0.0 g
Cholesterol	0 mg
Sodium	60 mg
Potassium	145 mg
Total Carbohydrate	6 g
Dietary Fiber	4 g
Sugars	1 g
Protein	1 g
Phosphorus	35 mg

Pan-Seared Pork Tenderloin with Sautéed Apples (page 92)

Shaved Raw Brussels Sprout Salad with Blueberries and Parmesan (page 2)

Spicy Miso Guacamole

SERVES 8

SERVING 1/4 cup

PREP 10 minutes

COOK 0 minutes

PAIRING SUGGESTION

Raw Zucchini Salad with Prunes (page 8) and Curry Shrimp with Peas (page 76)

INGREDIENTS

2 large ripe Hass avocados, halved, pitted, and peeled

Juice of 1 lime

1 teaspoon sriracha or other chili paste or sauce

1 teaspoon dark sesame oil

2 teaspoons shiro-miso

1 tablespoon minced red onion

1 1/2 tablespoons minced cilantro leaves

4 endives, white and/or red, leaves separated

Here is the popular Mexican guacamole with an Asian twist. Ever so slightly spicy, with an herbal note and a touch of miso, it will keep your dinner guests guessing. Chunky guacamole offers an interesting texture and gives the appearance of being super fresh. Smooth versions are also delicious, so have fun playing around with the texture. A delicious fruit loaded with vitamins and minerals, avocados provide a nutritious, good-for-you kind of fat, so take advantage. Served with endive leaves, this avocado dip makes for a healthy snack.

In a bowl, crush the avocado and mix in the lime juice, sriracha, sesame oil, miso, onion, and cilantro. Serve with endive leaves for dipping.

Miso pastes are made of fermented soybeans and available at better food markets, health food stores, and Asian markets. There are several types to choose from, from light to dark. The darker the miso, the saltier it is. Three types of miso are readily available; the most common and popular is called shiro-miso, so-called "white" miso, which is actually beige in color and less salty than the rest. It's ever so slightly sweet, which makes for a balanced flavor. Some miso types are grainy while others are smooth. A smooth-textured miso is best for this recipe.

1 Carbohydrate
1 Fat

Calories	110
Calories from Fat	65
Total Fat	7.0 g
Saturated Fat	1.0 g
Trans Fat	0.0 g
Cholesterol	0 mg
Sodium	85 mg
Potassium	820 mg
Total Carbohydrate	11 g
Dietary Fiber	9 g
Sugars	1 g
Protein	3 g
Phosphorus	80 mg

Raw Zucchini Salad with
Prunes (page 8)

Curry Shrimp with Peas
(page 76)

Carrot Salad with Coconut and Sunflower Seeds

SERVES 8

SERVING 1/2 cup

PREP 10 minutes

PAIRING SUGGESTION

Pan-Seared Pork Tenderloin with Sautéed Apples (page 92) and Baby Bok Choy Stir-Fried with Ginger and Garlic (page 18)

INGREDIENTS

3 cups shredded carrots

2 1/2 tablespoons unsweetened shredded coconut

2 tablespoons raw sunflower seeds

Juice of 1 lemon

2 tablespoons olive oil

Red pepper flakes to taste

Salt and pepper to taste

1/4 cup chopped cilantro leaves

One of the nicest combinations is carrot and coconut, believe it or not. A salad I once had at an Indian meal, it was refreshing simply dressed with lemon juice and a touch of olive oil, with salt and pepper. It was that simple.

In a bowl, toss together the carrots, coconut, sunflower seeds, lemon juice, and olive oil. Season with red pepper flakes and salt and pepper. Garnish with cilantro and serve.

EXCHANGES / CHOICES
1 Vegetable
1 Fat

Calories	70
Calories from Fat	55
Total Fat	6.0 g
Saturated Fat	1.5 g
Trans Fat	0.0 g
Cholesterol	0 mg
Sodium	30 mg
Potassium	150 mg
Total Carbohydrate	5 g
Dietary Fiber	2 g
Sugars	2 g
Protein	1 g
Phosphorus	35 mg

Pan-Seared Pork Tenderloin
with Sautéed Apples
(page 92)

Baby Bok Choy Stir-Fried
with Ginger and Garlic
(page 18)

Raw Kale and Roasted Sweet Potato Salad

SERVES 8

SERVING 2 cups

PREP 20 minutes

COOK 20 minutes

PAIRING SUGGESTION
Pan-Seared Scallops with
Avocado Walnut Sauce
(page 82)

INGREDIENTS

2 large sweet potatoes (or
    4 small ones), scrubbed and
    cut into bite-sized pieces
3 tablespoons grapeseed oil,
    divided use
1/2 teaspoon curry powder
1 tablespoon light soy sauce
1 teaspoon sriracha (optional)
1 teaspoon finely grated ginger
2 tablespoons rice vinegar
1 teaspoon dark sesame oil
1 bunch large kale leaves, ribs
    removed, and julienned
    (6 to 8 cups)

Kale has become popular over the last few years and touted as one of the healthiest foods on the planet. A great way to enjoy kale is raw as a salad. I've become a huge fan of these raw leaves, but the trick to keeping the rough chewing down to a minimum is to finely julienne the leaves or chop them and toss them in a salad dressing, allowing the leaves to macerate for 1 hour or so before serving. This tenderizes the leaves, and the longer they macerate, the softer they become. In other words, it's taking the rough out of roughage! Adding roasted sweet potatoes makes for an interesting flavor and texture combination, not to mention colorful presentation perfect for Thanksgiving dinner, for example.

1   Preheat the oven to 400°F for 20 minutes. In a bowl toss the sweet potatoes with 2 tablespoons grapeseed oil and the curry powder. Scatter on a baking sheet and roast until tender and golden, 15 to 20 minutes.

2   Meanwhile, in a medium to large bowl, whisk together the soy sauce, sriracha, ginger, and vinegar until well combined. Add the sesame oil and remaining grapeseed oil. Add the kale and toss well. When cooked, add the roasted sweet potatoes and serve.

EXCHANGES / CHOICES
1 Starch
1 Vegetable
1 Fat

Calories	135
Calories from Fat	55
Total Fat	6.0 g
Saturated Fat	0.6 g
Trans Fat	0.0 g
Cholesterol	0 mg
Sodium	110 mg
Potassium	570 mg
Total Carbohydrate	18 g
Dietary Fiber	3 g
Sugars	9 g
Protein	4 g
Phosphorus	90 mg

Pan-Seared Scallops with
Avocado Walnut Sauce
(page 82)

Raw Kale Salad with Tofu, Cherries, and Walnuts

SERVES 8

SERVING 1 1/2 cups

PREP 20 minutes

COOK 20 minutes

PAIRING SUGGESTION
Curry Split Pea Soup (page 38)

INGREDIENTS

4 tablespoons grapeseed oil, divided use

1 pound firm tofu, cut into bite-sized cubes (about 3/4 inch)

2 tablespoons rice vinegar

1 tablespoon soy sauce ("lite" soy sauce)

1 tablespoon freshly grated ginger

1 teaspoon sriracha or other hot sauce (optional)

1 tablespoon dark sesame oil

1 bunch kale, ribs removed, leaves julienned

1/3 cup dried tart cherries

1/3 cup chopped raw or dry-roasted unsalted walnuts

Tofu croutons, which are not only crispy on the outside but soft and tender on the inside, are a great source of protein. Here I use the dense regular, grainy-textured, firm tofu to make the croutons. For a healthy version of crispy tofu, pan-fry it in a nonstick skillet, keeping the oil down to a minimum. And, if you prefer, you can skip pan-crisping the tofu and simply add it to the salad fresh from the container, after draining it thoroughly. Also, unless a recipe specifically calls for "silken" tofu, you can assume that it calls for the regular type.

1. In a large nonstick skillet over medium heat, add 2 tablespoons grapeseed oil. Keeping the tofu cubes separated, pan-fry them until golden on all sides, about 5 minutes total. Drain on a paper towel–lined plate and set aside.

2. In a medium to large bowl, whisk together the vinegar, soy, ginger, and Sriracha until well combined. Whisk in the sesame oil and remaining grapeseed oil. Add the kale, toss well, and let stand for 15–20 minutes. Toss in the crispy tofu and serve garnished with dried cherries and walnuts.

Selecting tofu can be confusing. There are two basic readily available types: "silken," which is smooth like custard, and regular, which tends to be a bit grainy in texture. Each has its use. For example, the silken type is used in the popular Japanese miso soup. The Chinese most often use the regular grainy tofu for braising or frying. Within those two categories, there are subcategories such as "soft," "medium-firm," "firm," and "extra-firm." The firmer the tofu, the higher the fat content.

EXCHANGES / CHOICES
1/2 Carbohydrate
1 Protein, medium fat
2 Fat

Calories	190
Calories from Fat	125
Total Fat	14.0 g
Saturated Fat	1.7 g
Trans Fat	0.0 g
Cholesterol	0 mg
Sodium	90 mg
Potassium	315 mg
Total Carbohydrate	11 g
Dietary Fiber	2 g
Sugars	8 g
Protein	7 g
Phosphorus	160 mg

Curry Split Pea Soup
(page 38)

Tomato and Green Onion Salad

SERVES 8

SERVING 1/2 tomato (1/2 cup)

PREP 10 minutes

COOK 0 minutes

PAIRING SUGGESTION

Pan-Seared Scallops with Avocado Walnut Sauce (page 82)

INGREDIENTS

2 teaspoons Dijon mustard

2 tablespoons red wine vinegar

3 tablespoons olive oil

Salt and pepper to taste

4 medium ripe red tomatoes, sliced into thin rounds

2 scallions, trimmed and thinly sliced into rounds

A French classic, this tomato and green onion (aka "scallion") salad is so simple and refreshing you'll want to make it every summer when the fruit is in season and especially sweet. Bright red tomatoes or a mix of colorful heirloom varieties will give you delicious sweet and tangy results. One of my favorites is the komato tomato. You can slice the tomatoes into rounds, revealing the seeds in their sections, or dice them. In France, the tomatoes are sliced into thin rounds to absorb the dressing and make each bite delicate and tender. Be guided by the texture you desire.

1   In a small bowl, whisk together the mustard, vinegar, and oil, and season with salt and pepper.

2   In a shallow platter, arrange the tomatoes so they overlap. Scatter the scallions on top and drizzle with the dressing.

EXCHANGES / CHOICES
1 Vegetable
1 Fat

Calories	60
Calories from Fat	45
Total Fat	5.0 g
Saturated Fat	0.7 g
Trans Fat	0.0 g
Cholesterol	0 mg
Sodium	35 mg
Potassium	190 mg
Total Carbohydrate	3 g
Dietary Fiber	1 g
Sugars	2 g
Protein	1 g
Phosphorus	20 mg

Pan-Seared Scallops with
Avocado Walnut Sauce
(page 82)

Sautéed Mushrooms with Balsamic, Garlic, and Parsley

SERVES 8

SERVING 1/3 cup

PREP 10 minutes

COOK 5 minutes

PAIRING SUGGESTION

Oak Leaf Lettuce and Pear Salad with Stilton (page 4) and Rosemary-Sage Turkey Breast (page 90)

INGREDIENTS

2 tablespoons olive oil

3 large garlic cloves, crushed, peeled, and sliced

1 pound brown cap mushrooms, stems trimmed, quartered

1 tablespoon balsamic vinegar

Salt and pepper to taste

3 tablespoons finely chopped parsley leaves

Mushrooms are delicious all year round, but during the fall many varieties are available at the market. Look for oysters, trumpets, and porcini to make this delicious, simple sautéed mushroom dish, drizzled with balsamic and scented with garlic and parsley. Any mushroom, like the readily available baby brown or white caps and shiitake, can be used for this simple, hearty, and flavorful side dish, which complements all sorts of protein and vegetable entrées. Mushrooms, like leafy greens, are mostly water. They wilt and shrink quickly when cooked, so be sure to buy plenty.

In a skillet over medium heat, add the olive oil and sauté the garlic and mushrooms until tender, about 5 minutes. Add the balsamic, season with salt and pepper, and toss well. Serve, garnished generously with parsley.

EXCHANGES / CHOICES

1 Vegetable
1/2 Fat

Calories	45
Calories from Fat	30
Total Fat	3.5 g
Saturated Fat	0.5 g
Trans Fat	0.0 g
Cholesterol	0 mg
Sodium	0 mg
Potassium	265 mg
Total Carbohydrate	3 g
Dietary Fiber	0 g
Sugars	1 g
Protein	2 g
Phosphorus	70 mg

Oak Leaf Lettuce and Pear Salad with Stilton (page 4)

Rosemary-Sage Turkey Breast (page 90)

Roasted Beets & Leaves with Stilton

SERVES 8

SERVING 1/2 cup

PREP 10 minutes

COOK 40 minutes

PAIRING SUGGESTION
Turkey Vegetable Soup (page 46)

INGREDIENTS

3 large beets, scrubbed well and sliced into thin wedges or cubed (about 4 cups), beet leaves reserved with stems trimmed

2 tablespoons olive oil

Salt and pepper to taste

1/3 cup crumbled Stilton or other blue cheese

Is there anything more beautiful than deep red beets on a plate? If you see them with their green leafy tops, buy them and sauté the tops. They are absolutely delicious. I like to use them as a bed of greens to present the roasted beets on. They are absolutely delicious, too. Stilton or any blue cheese adds another dimension to roasted beets, but you can also use feta cheese as an alternative. A small amount will go a long way.

Preheat the oven to 400°F for 20 minutes. In a roasting pan, add beets and leaves, drizzle with olive oil, season with salt and pepper, and roast until tender, about 15 minutes for the leaves and 40 minutes for the beets. Transfer to a serving dish, layering the beets atop their leaves, and sprinkle with blue cheese.

EXCHANGES / CHOICES
2 Vegetable
1 Fat

Calories	85
Calories from Fat	45
Total Fat	5.0 g
Saturated Fat	1.5 g
Trans Fat	0.1 g
Cholesterol	5 mg
Sodium	180 mg
Potassium	395 mg
Total Carbohydrate	8 g
Dietary Fiber	3 g
Sugars	5 g
Protein	3 g
Phosphorus	55 mg

Turkey Vegetable Soup
(page 46)

SOUPS

Hot soups are delicious any time of the year. Thick or thin, in many cultures they are considered comfort and/or healing foods, warming the body while aiding digestion. I love cooking soup, the simmering sweet, savory, and spicy aromas permeating the air. There is nothing like a big bowl of soup during the fall, winter, or spring, taking the chill off the bones.

Thick legume-based soups are popular especially during the fall and winter when you need a little extra to fend off the chill. These soups take a while to cook to soften the beans or lentils, but I don't mind because I use this opportunity to warm up the house. I highly recommend building the flavors over several hours, softening the legumes while they take on the flavor of spices and foundational ingredients such as garlic, onion, celery, and carrots, for example. There is nothing like slow-cooking soups to maximize flavor. I also like to thin leftover bean, lentil, or pea soup with extra stock or water and drink it out of a mug on a snowy day. It's a flavorful vegetable infusion!

To soak or not to soak beans? I don't. Some swear by soaking beans at least 4 hours or overnight. It makes no difference. I simmer my bean soups an average of 10 to 12 hours. The same goes for lentils and peas. The result is a varied texture with a creamy consistency, some broken-down beans and some whole. The flavor is superior to any soup made with canned beans. And really, when soup simmers, you can go ahead and do your house chores, read a book, or listen to music. Nothing lost, everything gained!

Included in this section is also a Japanese restaurant classic, miso soup. At its base is shiro-miso, a beige-colored fermented bean paste, the main flavor of this delicious and light soup. Unlike bean soups, it takes only 5 to 10 minutes to make and is packed with seaweed flavor. Don't let the ingredients scare you. They are all readily available in many supermarkets now and most certainly in your local health food store. Broths are especially wonderful to sip at the end or throughout a meal to aid digestion. Once you see how easy miso soup is to make, there is no doubt it will quickly become one of your favorite recipes. I love to add all sorts of ingredients like cucumber, mushrooms, baby spinach leaves, or fresh peas to this basic broth.

With a few exceptions, the only way to make most soups is in large batches because reheating them only enhances the flavors. Take pleasure in making soups ahead of time, using only the freshest, healthiest ingredients. For convenience, you can store leftovers in containers and freeze them for up to 3 months.

Curry Split
Pea Soup

SERVES 8

SERVING 1 cup

PREP 15 minutes

COOK 3 hours
15 minutes

PAIRING SUGGESTION

Fennel Salad with Blood Orange
(page 6) and Apple Cranberry
Pecan Crisp (page 100)

INGREDIENTS

2 tablespoons olive oil

1 medium onion (yellow, white,
or red), peeled and finely
chopped

4 large garlic cloves, peeled and
crushed

4 medium to large carrots,
peeled and chopped

1 tablespoon curry powder

1 pound dried split peas

Salt and pepper to taste

Split pea soup is an American favorite and oftentimes is made with bits of bacon. Not exactly the healthiest thing to add to soups, but flavorful for sure. Replace the bacon with curry powder and you have yourself a truly healthy, guilt-free version of split pea soup packed with exotic spices and sweetened only with the natural flavors of caramelized onion, garlic, and carrots. This will quickly become a family favorite. Look for a consistency that is not too thick and not too thin. Make it light, but substantial and flavorful.

In a large soup pot over medium heat, add the oil and sauté the onion, garlic, and carrots until golden, about 10 minutes, occasionally stirring. Stir in the curry powder and sauté for 2 minutes more. Add the split peas and continue to stir for 2 minutes until a shade darker. Add 3 quarts of water and bring to a boil. Reduce the heat to medium-low, partially cover the pot, and continue to cook stirring occasionally, until reduced by half and thickened, about 3 hours. Season lightly with salt and pepper, stir and serve hot, or store for up to a week in the refrigerator or 3 months in the freezer.

Every stove is different. Be sure to check the soup occasionally and stir the ingredients to prevent any burning, especially with electric stoves where you might experience hot spots. And feel free to add water in case it evaporates too quickly.

Curry powders are not all created equal. Some are spicier and/or saltier than others. Be sure you taste before adjusting the seasoning of your recipe with salt and pepper.

EXCHANGES / CHOICES
2 Starch
1 Vegetable
1 Protein, lean

Calories	225
Calories from Fat	35
Total Fat	4.0 g
Saturated Fat	0.6 g
Trans Fat	0.0 g
Cholesterol	0 mg
Sodium	25 mg
Potassium	660 mg
Total Carbohydrate	36 g
Dietary Fiber	13 g
Sugars	6 g
Protein	13 g
Phosphorus	165 mg

Fennel Salad with Blood
Orange (page 6)

Apple Cranberry Pecan
Crisp (page 100)

Smoked Tomato Bean Soup

SERVES 8

SERVING 1 cup

PREP 15 minutes

COOK 1 hour

PAIRING SUGGESTION
Shaved Raw Brussels Sprout Salad with Blueberries and Parmesan (page 2)

INGREDIENTS
2 tablespoons olive oil

1 large onion, peeled and minced

4 large garlic cloves, peeled and minced

3 celery sticks, chopped

3 medium to large carrots, peeled and chopped

1 green bell pepper, stem and seeds removed, and chopped

1 tablespoon smoked paprika

1 teaspoon ground cumin

2 tablespoons dried oregano

One 28-ounce can crushed tomatoes

4 cups cooked cannellini beans, kidney, or other beans (or 1 pound uncooked dried beans)

3 quarts low-sodium vegetable stock

1/2 cup cilantro leaves (garnish)

In a pinch you can make a great soup with tomatoes and beans. A little smoked paprika, some oregano and cumin and you have something similar to classic chili without the heaviness of meat yet just as hearty.

In a large heavy-bottom pot over medium heat, add the oil and sauté the onions and garlic until golden, about 5 minutes. Add the celery, carrots, and pepper and continue to cook until caramelized, about 10 minutes. Add the paprika, cumin, and oregano, and stir a few times until well distributed. Add the tomatoes, beans, and stock. Season with salt and pepper, if desired, and lower heat to simmer and cook, covered, until the beans are broken down and the juices are thickened, about 45 minutes. Garnish with cilantro leaves.

You can use all sorts of beans, red, kidney, black, pinto, or whatever you have on hand. You can even mix them together for an interesting texture for all beans break down differently.

For an even heartier soup, add 1 pound of lean ground beef or turkey after caramelizing the onions and garlic, sautéing the meat until cooked through, separated, and lightly golden, about 10 minutes. Then proceed with the recipe.

EXCHANGES / CHOICES
1 1/2 Starch
3 Vegetable
1 Fat

Calories	235	
Calories from Fat	40	
Total Fat	4.5	g
Saturated Fat	0.6	g
Trans Fat	0.0	g
Cholesterol	0	mg
Sodium	380	mg
Potassium	1100	mg
Total Carbohydrate	40	g
Dietary Fiber	12	g
Sugars	11	g
Protein	10	g
Phosphorus	305	mg

Shaved Raw Brussels Sprout
Salad with Blueberries and
Parmesan (page 2)

Butternut Squash Soup with Pine Nuts and Goji Berries

SERVES 8

SERVING 1 cup

PREP 15 minutes

COOK 35 minutes

PAIRING SUGGESTION

Avocado, Corn, and Tomato Salad (page 60) and Dates, Baby Arugula, and Stilton (page 106)

INGREDIENTS

2 cups low-fat unsweetened coconut milk drink

1 large butternut squash, peeled, seeded, and roughly cubed (4 to 5 cups)

1 teaspoon curry powder

Salt and pepper to taste

1/4 cup toasted pine nuts

1/4 cup goji berries (optional)

The fall is a great time of year when all sorts of winter squash are available at the market, including butternut. Bright orange, its flesh is naturally sweet and makes for a smooth, silky soup that's thick or thin or somewhere in between depending on your preference. With a touch of coconut milk and a hint of curry, it is one of those soothing, satisfying soups that can be had as a complete meal with freshly tossed salad greens on the side. It's also wonderful as a first course to a celebratory meal or any holiday.

In a medium pot over medium-low heat add the coconut milk, 2 cups water, butternut squash, and curry powder. Cook until the squash is tender, about 30 minutes. Working in batches as needed, transfer the soup to a blender and process until smooth. Return to pot and season with salt and pepper. Bring to a gentle boil and serve hot, garnished with pine nuts and goji berries, if using.

A great substitute for butternut squash is pink pumpkin or kabocha squash, aka "Japanese pumpkin." The results will be slightly different, sweeter, and perhaps a little smoother. These pumpkins may even give you a slightly thicker version of the soup, but that is also partly a function of how much liquid you add to the pot for the desired consistency. There is no rule other than it should be delicious!

EXCHANGES / CHOICES

1/2 Starch
1 Fat

Calories	75
Calories from Fat	40
Total Fat	4.5 g
Saturated Fat	1.5 g
Trans Fat	0.0 g
Cholesterol	0 mg
Sodium	10 mg
Potassium	280 mg
Total Carbohydrate	10 g
Dietary Fiber	3 g
Sugars	2 g
Protein	2 g
Phosphorus	55 mg

Avocado, Corn, and Tomato
Salad (page 60)

Date, Baby Arugula, and
Stilton (page 106)

Carrot Ginger Soup with Parsley

SERVES 8

SERVING I cup

PREP I5 minutes

COOK 30 minutes

PAIRING SUGGESTION
White Bean Salad with Golden Garlic Oil (page 68) and Berries with Balsamic and Fresh Basil (page 98)

INGREDIENTS
2 pounds of carrots, peeled

2 tablespoons olive oil

2 ounces ginger, peeled, finely grated, and juiced (if desired)

Salt and pepper to taste

1/2 cup chopped parsley

Carrots are one of those inexpensive root vegetables that often show up grated in salads. Though carrot ginger soup has become a popular combination over the years, this version is especially tasty because the carrots are roasted until caramelized. It adds a layer of flavor that you would not otherwise get were you to simply boil the carrots.

1 Preheat the oven to 400°F for 20 minutes. Scatter the carrots on a baking sheet and brush them with olive oil. Roast until tender and caramelized, about 20 minutes.

2 Working in batches if necessary, transfer the carrots to a blender with 4 cups of water. Process until smooth and pour into a heavy-bottom pot. Bring to a light boil over medium heat, and reduce to simmer. Add the ginger and season with salt and pepper. Garnish each serving with some chopped parsley.

To juice fresh ginger, finely grate the rhizome, place the pulp in a cheese cloth, and squeeze the juice over a bowl until the pulp runs out and is dried up. Alternatively, use a juicer if you plan on juicing large quantities, or skip this part altogether if you don't mind grated pulp in the soup.

EXCHANGES / CHOICES
2 Vegetable
1/2 Fat

Calories	80
Calories from Fat	30
Total Fat	3.5 g
Saturated Fat	0.5 g
Trans Fat	0.0 g
Cholesterol	0 mg
Sodium	75 mg
Potassium	370 mg
Total Carbohydrate	11 g
Dietary Fiber	3 g
Sugars	5 g
Protein	1 g
Phosphorus	40 mg

White Bean Salad with
Golden Garlic Oil
(page 68)

Berries with Balsamic and
Fresh Basil (page 98)

Turkey Vegetable Soup

SERVES 8

SERVING 1 cup

PREP 30 minutes

COOK 2 hours

PAIRING SUGGESTION
Vegetable and Mushroom
Frittata (page 74)

INGREDIENTS

2 tablespoons olive oil

4 large garlic cloves, crushed
and peeled

4 leeks, trimmed and cut into
bite-size pieces

6 sticks celery, cut into bite-size
pieces

6 medium to large carrots, peeled
and cut into bite-size pieces

1/2 small to medium daikon or
rutabaga, peeled and cut into
bite-size pieces

1 pound brown cap button
mushrooms, stems trimmed,
halved or quartered

1 pound Brussels sprouts, trimmed
and halved or quartered

1/2 leftover or roasted turkey
breast, skin and visible fat
removed, meat shredded

10 sprigs parsley, stems trimmed

1 large sprig rosemary

1 large sprig sage

Salt and pepper to taste

Leftover Thanksgiving turkey is fantastic for making soup, a comfort food many look forward to during the cold months. There's usually plenty of meat to make a large batch of soothing broth loaded with chunky vegetables. Keep it in your freezer in small containers and make it last throughout the winter. The shredded turkey meat called for in the recipe can easily come from the meaty bones, which is where the meat is the most flavorful.

In a large stockpot over medium heat, add the oil and sauté the garlic, leeks, celery, and carrots until golden, about 20 minutes. Fill the pot with 4 quarts water and add the daikon, mushrooms, Brussels sprouts, turkey, parsley, rosemary, and sage. Bring to a boil and reduce heat to medium-low, season with salt and pepper, and cook until reduced by 1 1/2 quarts, about 1 1/2 to 2 hours. Serve soup, discarding bones in the process.

Substitute the same amount of leftover roast chicken for the turkey.

Soups can be refrigerated for up to 3 days or frozen for up to 3 months.

EXCHANGES / CHOICES
4 Vegetable
3 Protein, lean

Calories	235
Calories from Fat	40
Total Fat	4.5 g
Saturated Fat	0.8 g
Trans Fat	0.0 g
Cholesterol	70 mg
Sodium	140 mg
Potassium	1100 mg
Total Carbohydrate	21 g
Dietary Fiber	6 g
Sugars	7 g
Protein	30 g
Phosphorus	340 mg

Vegetable and Mushroom
Frittata (page 74)

Miso Soup with Crispy Tofu and Refreshing Cucumber

SERVES 8

SERVING 1 cup

PREP 15 minutes

COOK 35 minutes

PAIRING SUGGESTION

Brown Rice & Broccoli Salad with Nuts and Seeds (page 52) and Curry Shrimp with Peas (page 76)

INGREDIENTS

2 tablespoons grapeseed oil

1 pound firm tofu, cut into 3/4-inch cubes

2 quarts spring water

One piece dried kombu (kelp) seaweed, 2 × 4 inches, wiped

1/3 cup sake (optional)

1/2 cup shiro-miso (smooth in texture, preferably)

1/2 hothouse cucumber, peeled and cut into 1/2-inch cubes

2 ounces fresh ginger (about 2-inch-long piece), peeled and grated (optional)

1 1/2 tablespoons dark sesame oil (optional)

2 tablespoons wakame, soaked in water until pliable, chopped if necessary

4 scallions, trimmed and paper-thinly sliced

There is nothing easier to make than Japanese miso soup, and it can take less than 5 minutes of cooking time. Most of the flavor comes from the shiro-miso, or fermented "white" soybean paste. Here, a vegetarian version using kombu, kelp seaweed, is used to enhance the flavor of the stock, along with some sake wine. The addition of cucumber is also very refreshing and the crunchiness of pan-crisped tofu is an unexpected bonus. Enjoy this basic recipe for miso soup, with optional ingredients for added texture and flavor.

1 In a medium nonstick pan over medium heat, add the oil and tofu, separating the pieces. Cook the tofu until crispy on every side, about 5 minutes, flipping each piece every minute or so.

2 In the meantime, in a medium stockpot, add the spring water, kombu, sake, and miso. Bring to a gentle boil over medium heat, then reduce to low. Whisk until the miso paste is completely dissolved. Simmer for 30 minutes until the broth takes on the flavor of the kombu. Add the cucumber, ginger, and sesame oil, and cook for 2 minutes more. To serve, add a few crispy tofu cubes and tablespoon wakame to each serving. Ladle 1 cup miso soup with cucumber over each serving, and garnish with some scallions.

Think of miso soup as a basic broth, to which you can add all sorts of ingredients like mushrooms, sliced meats, seafood, vegetables, and soba noodles, for example. Once you know how to make the basic broth, the possibilities are endless. Treat it like any other broth.

Kombu stock is easy to make. Place a 2 × 4-inch kombu piece in 2 quarts of spring water and let stand overnight on your kitchen counter at room temperature. The next morning you have kombu stock, or you can simply add the kombu to the stockpot, in a pinch.

EXCHANGES / CHOICES
1/2 Carbohydrate
1 Protein, lean
1/2 Fat

Calories	105
Calories from Fat	55
Total Fat	6.0 g
Saturated Fat	0.8 g
Trans Fat	0.0 g
Cholesterol	0 mg
Sodium	365 mg
Potassium	145 mg
Total Carbohydrate	8 g
Dietary Fiber	2 g
Sugars	5 g
Protein	6 g
Phosphorus	105 mg

Brown Rice & Broccoli
Salad with Nuts and Seeds
(page 52)

Curry Shrimp with Peas
(page 76)

WHOLE GRAINS & LEGUMES

Everyone needs something that sticks to the ribs, but in small, sensible doses. In this chapter you'll find all sorts of grains and legumes, the type of food that acts as a canvas upon which all sorts of vegetable, meat, and seafood dishes can add color, texture, and flavor. Starchy and/or rich, grains and legumes are excellent anytime of the year; they can also easily be prepared ahead of time and refrigerated for up to 3 days. Eat them hot, at room temperature, or lightly chilled depending on the season.

While beans take a long time to cook, I recommend that you start with your dried beans rather than the canned version. If you do use canned beans, be sure to rinse them well to remove excess sodium (salt), boil them submerged in water for 5 minutes, drain well, and then use them in the recipes that follow.

Beans, lentils, and dried peas take 2–3 hours to cook. During the cooking process, be sure to replenish the pot with water as necessary so as to completely submerge the beans at all times. Also, cook the beans until they are tender all the way through. Tough beans are tough on the stomach! Remember that not all beans are created equal. Some will break apart while others will remain whole when done.

Brown Rice & Broccoli Salad with Nuts and Seeds

SERVES 8

SERVING 1 cup

PREP 15 minutes

COOK 40 minutes

PAIRING SUGGESTION

Broiled Miso Salmon (page 80) and Baby Bok Choy Stir-Fried with Ginger and Garlic (page 18)

Brown rice is rich in fiber and delicious, giving food a nutty, wholesome flavor. Tossed with raw broccoli, nuts, and seeds, this rice dish makes for a highly nutritious side or salad topping.

INGREDIENTS

2 cups freshly cooked brown rice

1 1/2 cups shaved broccoli heads

2 tablespoons raw pumpkin seeds

2 tablespoons raw sunflower seeds

1/3 cup crushed walnuts

1/2 cup dried tart cherries

Juice of 1 lemon

1 1/2 tablespoons lower-sodium soy sauce

1 1/2 tablespoons olive oil

1 teaspoon dark sesame oil

1 teaspoon sriracha or other hot sauce

In a large bowl, add the brown rice, broccoli, pumpkin and sunflower seeds, walnuts, cherries, lemon juice, soy sauce, olive and sesame oils, and sriracha. Toss well and serve.

To shave broccoli heads, hold by the stem and slice across the florets creating "green dust." For the rice, be sure to boil it in plain water without salt, butter, or oil, which is the traditional Asian style.

EXCHANGES / CHOICES
1 Starch
1/2 Fruit
1 1/2 Fat

Calories	180
Calories from Fat	80
Total Fat	9.0 g
Saturated Fat	1.1 g
Trans Fat	0.0 g
Cholesterol	0 mg
Sodium	125 mg
Potassium	165 mg
Total Carbohydrate	22 g
Dietary Fiber	3 g
Sugars	8 g
Protein	4 g
Phosphorus	165 mg

Broiled Miso Salmon
(page 80)

Baby Bok Choy Stir-Fried
with Ginger and Garlic
(page 18)

Tabbouleh with Cucumber and Tomatoes

SERVES 8

SERVING 1 cup

PREP 15 minutes

COOK 45 minutes

PAIRING SUGGESTION

Spicy Lemon-Sesame Hummus (page 66) and White Bean Salad with Golden Garlic Oil (page 68)

INGREDIENTS

1/3 cup fine bulgur

1 large bunch parsley, flat or curly, leaves only, finely chopped (about 1 1/2 cups)

1/2 bunch sprigs mint, leaves only, finely julienned (about 1/2 cup)

1/2 hothouse cucumber, peeled, seeded, and cut into 1/2-inch dice

8 cherry tomatoes, diced

Juice of 1 lemon

1 tablespoon olive oil

Salt and pepper to taste

A traditional dish in Middle Eastern cuisines, tabbouleh is mostly parsley and mint with just a touch of bulgur, which is cracked wheat, for added chewy texture. Like most "classic" and "authentic" dishes in the world, there are as many variations of tabbouleh as there are regions and cooks, with more or less bulgur in the mix, although more herbs are definitely healthier and more refreshing than more bulgur.

In a large bowl, add the bulgur and 1/2 cup hot water. Cover and let rest for 30 minutes. Fluff with fork and add the parsley, mint, cucumber, cherry tomatoes, lemon juice, olive oil, and salt and pepper. Toss well, let stand for 15 minutes, and serve.

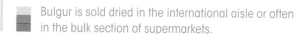

Bulgur is sold dried in the international aisle or often in the bulk section of supermarkets.

EXCHANGES / CHOICES
1/2 Starch

Calories	45
Calories from Fat	20
Total Fat	2.0 g
Saturated Fat	0.3 g
Trans Fat	0.0 g
Cholesterol	0 mg
Sodium	10 mg
Potassium	150 mg
Total Carbohydrate	7 g
Dietary Fiber	2 g
Sugars	1 g
Protein	1 g
Phosphorus	35 mg

Spicy Lemon-Sesame
Hummus (page 66)

White Bean Salad with
Golden Garlic Oil (page 68)

Quinoa with Kale and Dried Cranberries

SERVES 8

SERVING 1 cup

PREP 15 minutes

COOK 25 minutes

PAIRING SUGGESTION
Crab Cakes with Parsnip Purée
(page 84)

INGREDIENTS
3 tablespoons olive oil, divided
    use
1/2 cup red quinoa, rinsed and
    drained (about 1 1/2 cups
    cooked)
1 1/4 cups water
1 scallion, trimmed and minced
Juice of 1 lemon
Salt and pepper to taste
4 to 5 leaves kale, finely
    chopped (about 2 cups)
1/2 cup low-salt feta, crumbled
1/3 cup dried cranberries, finely
    chopped

Contrary to popular belief, quinoa is a seed, not a grain. High in protein and fiber and naturally gluten-free, quinoa is light and perfect for salads. Feel free to use red, black, or white quinoa for this feta and raw kale salad.

1 In a small pot over medium heat, add 1 tablespoon oil and toast the quinoa lightly. Add the water and bring to a boil. Reduce heat to medium-low and cook, covered, until the water is completely absorbed, 15–20 minutes. Let stand for 5 minutes, and then fluff with fork.

2 Meanwhile, in a salad bowl add the scallion, lemon juice, remaining olive oil, kale, and quinoa. Toss well and serve, garnished with feta and cranberries.

EXCHANGES / CHOICES
1/2 Starch
1/2 Fruit
1 1/2 Fat

Calories	135	
Calories from Fat	65	
Total Fat	7.0	g
Saturated Fat	1.5	g
Trans Fat	0.0	g
Cholesterol	5	mg
Sodium	115	mg
Potassium	160	mg
Total Carbohydrate	14	g
Dietary Fiber	2	g
Sugars	6	g
Protein	5	g
Phosphorus	100	mg

Crab Cakes with Parsnip
Purée (page 84)

Black Bean and Red Bell Pepper Salad

SERVES 8

SERVING 3/4 cup

PREP 15 minutes

COOK 10 minutes

PAIRING SUGGESTION

Pan-Seared Scallops with
Avocado Walnut Sauce
(page 82)

INGREDIENTS

2 tablespoons olive oil

2 red bell peppers, peeled and
chopped

1 medium red onion, peeled and
chopped

4 cups freshly cooked black
beans, drained thoroughly

Juice and zest of 1 lime

2 teaspoons shiro-miso

1/2 teaspoon sriracha or other
hot sauce

1 teaspoon ginger juice

I love bean salads, serving them at room temperature or hot depending on the season. Here the combination of black beans tossed with vibrant sautéed red bell peppers and red onions makes for a beautiful festive presentation. This is one of those simple salads that you can experiment with easily. For instance, if you don't have black beans, use whatever beans you have on hand. The dressing is very easy to make as well, using the now readily available shiro-miso, or white soybean paste.

1 In a large skillet over medium heat, add 2 tablespoons oil and sauté the bell peppers and onions until golden, about 7 minutes. Transfer to a serving bowl, add the black beans, and toss.

2 In a small bowl, whisk together the lime juice, miso, sriracha, and ginger juice. Drizzle over the black bean salad and garnish with lime zest.

 To make ginger juice, simply grate some ginger and place the pulp in the palm of your hand, then squeeze out the juice into a small bowl.

EXCHANGES / CHOICES

1 1/2 Starch
1 Vegetable
1 Fat

Calories	195	
Calories from Fat	65	
Total Fat	7.0	g
Saturated Fat	1.1	g
Trans Fat	0.0	g
Cholesterol	0	mg
Sodium	40	mg
Potassium	415	mg
Total Carbohydrate	25	g
Dietary Fiber	9	g
Sugars	5	g
Protein	8	g
Phosphorus	140	mg

Pan-Seared Scallops with
Avocado Walnut Sauce
(page 82)

Avocado, Corn, and Tomato Salad

SERVES 8

SERVING 3/4 cup

PREP 15 minutes

COOK 0 minutes

PAIRING SUGGESTION

Spicy Miso Guacamole
(page 22) and Pork Lettuce
Wrap with Prune Relish
(page 94)

INGREDIENTS

2 cups fresh corn kernels

2 cups sweet cherry tomatoes

2 ripe Hass avocados, halved,
     pitted, and cut into bite-size
     chunks

8 to 10 large mint leaves,
     julienned

2 tablespoons rice vinegar

1 tablespoon olive oil

Salt and pepper to taste

This recipe screams summer, the best time of year
for sweet juicy corn and tomatoes. A raw salad,
it is refreshing and colorful, combining fruit and
grain all in one. Corn is grain, so no need to double
up on carbs! Another added bonus is that avocado
is high in protein, which makes this nutrient-rich
recipe the perfect one-dish meal. This salad is best
served at room temperature, but you can also serve
it lightly chilled.

In a medium bowl, add the corn, tomatoes,
avocados, mint leaves, rice vinegar, olive oil, salt, and
pepper. Toss gently so as not to crush the avocado.

EXCHANGES / CHOICES
1 Carbohydrate
1 1/2 Fat

Calories	120
Calories from Fat	70
Total Fat	8.0 g
Saturated Fat	1.2 g
Trans Fat	0.0 g
Cholesterol	0 mg
Sodium	10 mg
Potassium	385 mg
Total Carbohydrate	12 g
Dietary Fiber	4 g
Sugars	3 g
Protein	2 g
Phosphorus	65 mg

Spicy Miso Guacamole
(page 22)

Pork Lettuce Wrap with
Prune Relish (page 94)

Veggie Burger with Pickled Red Onions

SERVES 8

SERVING 1 burger

PREP 30 minutes

COOK 20 minutes

PAIRING SUGGESTION

Oak Leaf Lettuce and Pear Salad with Stilton (page 4) and Berries with Balsamic and Fresh Basil (page 98)

INGREDIENTS

1 large red onion, peeled and sliced paper thin

1/3 cup white balsamic vinegar or rice vinegar

Salt to taste

3 tablespoons olive oil, divided use

1 large clove garlic, peeled and minced

1 small onion, peeled and finely chopped

1 large carrot, peeled and finely chopped

1 stick celery, trimmed and finely chopped

3 cups soft-cooked Puys lentils, drained thoroughly (water completely squeezed out)

12 sprigs thyme, leaves only except for 8 sprigs left intact for garnish

1/4 teaspoon cumin powder

Pepper to taste

Veggie burgers are one of the most popular items on the menu of vegetarian or vegan restaurants and increasingly so in non-vegetarian eateries as well. This one is made with French lentilles du Puys. While they are readily available, if you cannot find them, use any other lentil, cooking them until really soft in order to easily mix the ingredients and shape them into patties. The pickled red onion is easy to make and adds a sweet, sour, and mildly spicy flavor to the dish. Serve on buns, or simply as is for a more elegant entrée.

1 In a small bowl, add the sliced onion, separating the rings. Add the vinegar and season with salt. Toss well and let stand for 30 minutes.

2 In the meantime, in a large skillet over medium heat, add 1 tablespoon oil and sauté the garlic and minced onions until caramelized, about 2 minutes. Add the carrots and celery and continue to sauté until soft, about 10 minutes. Let cool.

3 In a medium mixing bowl, add the sautéed vegetables, lentils, thyme, and cumin. Season with salt and pepper and mash the ingredients together until well combined. Shape them into 4 large or 8 small round patties. In a large skillet over medium heat, add the remaining oil and pan-crisp the veggie burgers until crisp on the outside, about 5 minutes, flipping them once. Serve each patty, topped with some pickled red onion and garnished with a sprig of thyme.

Whether you're cooking beans or lentils, it doesn't matter how much water goes in the pot as long as the ingredients are submerged. A good rule of thumb is 4 times as much water as beans or lentils in the pot. This way you can allow for slow simmering for roughly 2 hours depending on the type of bean or lentil. Then drain and proceed with your recipe. The most important thing to remember is to cook them until tender. If beans are too firm, they will be difficult to digest.

EXCHANGES / CHOICES
1 Starch
1 Vegetable
1 Protein, lean
1/2 Fat

Calories	165
Calories from Fat	45
Total Fat	5.0 g
Saturated Fat	0.8 g
Trans Fat	0.0 g
Cholesterol	0 mg
Sodium	15 mg
Potassium	400 mg
Total Carbohydrate	22 g
Dietary Fiber	7 g
Sugars	5 g
Protein	7 g
Phosphorus	155 mg

Oak Leaf Lettuce and Pear
Salad with Stilton (page 4)

Berries with Balsamic and
Fresh Basil (page 98)

Curry-Spiced Pickled String Beans

SERVES 8

SERVING 1/3 cup (6 beans)

PREP 10 minutes

COOK O minutes

INGREDIENTS

2 cups rice vinegar

1 tablespoon salt

1 1/2 tablespoons agave nectar

2 teaspoons curry powder

1 ounce (1-inch piece) ginger, sliced lengthwise

1 pound string beans, ends trimmed

6 large garlic cloves, crushed and peeled

There's nothing easier than pickling and preserving all sorts of vegetables to snack on or to have as a table condiment to accompany any meal. It's especially wonderful with meat and seafood as a counterpoint to the richness of these proteins.

1 In a bowl whisk together the vinegar, salt, agave, curry powder, and ginger until the salt is dissolved completely.

2 In a clean, preferably sterilized quart jar, add the string beans, arranging them upright, sticking the garlic cloves, here and there. Pour the curry pickling liquid on top, cover, refrigerate, and let macerate for 1 week or longer.

Rice vinegar comes either unseasoned, therefore regular, or "seasoned" with salt and sugar. Choose the unseasoned version so you have control over the seasoning, including how much salt and sugar you add to pickling liquids, salad dressings, and other sauces.

EXCHANGES / CHOICES
1 Vegetable

Calories	25	
Calories from Fat	0	
Total Fat	0.0	g
Saturated Fat	0.0	g
Trans Fat	0.0	g
Cholesterol	0	mg
Sodium	120	mg
Potassium	125	mg
Total Carbohydrate	5	g
Dietary Fiber	1	g
Sugars	2	g
Protein	1	g
Phosphorus	25	mg

Spicy Lemon-Sesame Hummus

SERVES 8

SERVING 1/4 cup

PREP 10 minutes

COOK 0 minutes

PAIRING SUGGESTION

Tomato and Green Onion Salad (page 30) and Rosemary-Sage Turkey Breast (page 90)

INGREDIENTS

2 cups cooked chickpeas, skins removed, cooking water reserved

Juice of 2 lemons (about 1/2 cup)

1–2 large garlic cloves, peeled and grated

4 tablespoons olive oil, divided use

1 teaspoon dark sesame oil (optional)

1 teaspoon sriracha or hot sauce (optional)

Salt to taste

2 tablespoons finely chopped parsley

Pinch paprika (smoked or regular)

Hummus has become a popular food that is sold in any number of prepackaged flavor variations. Like all packaged foods, however, oftentimes they are loaded with preservatives. The recipe is so simple that it's worth making from scratch. Here is a simple recipe with some optional ingredients to create flavor variations. Feel free to add your own touch as well. Serve with crudité as a snack, meal, or starter.

In a food processor, add the chickpeas, lemon juice, garlic, 3 tablespoons olive oil, 1/3 cup reserved cooking liquid, and sesame oil and sriracha, if using. Season with salt and process until smooth or almost smooth, depending on desired texture. Transfer to a serving dish, garnish with parsley, and sprinkle with paprika. Drizzle the remaining olive oil on top and serve.

Like beans and lentils, cook dried chickpeas submerged in water until tender (about 2 hours) and the skins will then come off effortlessly. To remove skins from chickpeas, simply drain them from their cooking water (reserving the water), and soak them in cold water. Rub the chickpeas with your hands. The skins will come off easily and float to the top. Simply discard the skins. Drain chickpeas and proceed with recipe.

1 Starch
1 1/2 Fat

Calories	130
Calories from Fat	70
Total Fat	8.0 g
Saturated Fat	1.0 g
Trans Fat	0.0 g
Cholesterol	0 mg
Sodium	5 mg
Potassium	140 mg
Total Carbohydrate	12 g
Dietary Fiber	3 g
Sugars	2 g
Protein	4 g
Phosphorus	70 mg

Tomato and Green Onion Salad (page 30)

Rosemary-Sage Turkey Breast (page 90)

White Bean Salad with Golden Garlic Oil

SERVES 8

SERVING 1 cup

PREP 15 minutes

COOK 2 minutes

PAIRING SUGGESTION
Ratatouille (page 10) and
Apple Cranberry Pecan Crisp
(page 100)

INGREDIENTS
2 tablespoons olive oil
2 large garlic cloves, peeled and
    minced
4 cups cooked white beans,
    rinsed and drained
2 ripe Hass avocados, halved,
    pitted, peeled, and cut into
    bite-sized chunks
Juice of 1 lemon
Salt and pepper to taste

This white bean salad is both easy to make and really tasty, providing a great amount of fiber and protein in a balanced and healthy meal. Here I use white beans and toss them with creamy avocado and a generous amount of golden garlic oil. Simple, it not only replaces animal protein, but is so filling. Serve the beans warm or lightly chilled as an entree over a bed of fresh leafy greens.

1 In a small pan over medium heat, add the olive oil and garlic and cook until the garlic turns a light golden, about 2 minutes. Remove from heat.

2 In a large bowl, toss the beans and avocado. Add the lemon juice and season with salt and pepper. Toss a few more times and serve, drizzled with the garlic and its oil.

High in fiber and protein, beans are one of the best foods to have on hand. Inexpensive, they can be bought in bulk and are easy to cook. Just boil them for 2–3 hours until soft to the core. Cooked beans can last up to 3 days refrigerated and 3 months frozen and can be easily reheated. If canned beans are your only option, rinse the canned beans well, put them in a pot with water and boil them for 5 minutes prior to using them in a recipe.

1 1/2 Starch
1 Protein, lean
1 Fat

Calories	200
Calories from Fat	80
Total Fat	9.0 g
Saturated Fat	1.3 g
Trans Fat	0.0 g
Cholesterol	0 mg
Sodium	95 mg
Potassium	540 mg
Total Carbohydrate	24 g
Dietary Fiber	8 g
Sugars	1 g
Protein	8 g
Phosphorus	145 mg

Ratatouille (page 10)

Apple Cranberry Pecan Crisp (page 100)

EGGS, SEAFOOD, & MEAT

Meat and seafood protein should be enjoyed somewhat sparingly. For this reason, a 3- to 4-ounce portion is generally plenty. Also consider breaking up the week and replacing animal protein with highly nutritious legumes such as beans and lentils, which are not only a great source of protein but of fiber as well.

You will find this chapter to be smaller than the previous ones for good measure. Your vegetable intake should be considerably higher than your meat or fish protein intake. As a general rule, be sure that your meals are about 70% vegetarian and you'll be on your way to a healthier lifestyle, kicking up your energy level and increasing your metabolism, as you start feeling light on your feet.

While eggs and seafood are relatively low in fat, meat such as poultry, turkey, and pork have so many different cuts to choose from that I've stuck to those that are at least 70% lean, skipping beef altogether though including it as an option for those who love red meat. It's good practice to go for leaner, easier to digest cuts, and as you develop a conscious eating practice at home, you'll find yourself making similar selections in restaurants, opting for leaner, less calorie-laden cuts.

Enjoy this chapter loaded with easy-to-prepare, healthful seafood, poultry, and meat recipes that can be made ahead to save time. Additionally, the marinades, sauces, and herb pastes can be used with any number of meat or fish proteins, so feel free to experiment in the kitchen.

Baked Eggs with Ratatouille and Parmesan

SERVES 8

SERVING 1 egg and 1/2 cup ratatouille

PREP 15 minutes

COOK 5 minutes

PAIRING SUGGESTION
Quinoa with Kale and Dried Cranberries (page 56)

INGREDIENTS
4 cups leftover Ratatouille
    (page 10)
16 large basil leaves, freshly torn
8 large eggs (1 per person)
1/2 cup grated Parmesan
    cheese (optional)
Pepper to taste

This braised vegetable specialty with zucchini, bell peppers, eggplant, tomatoes, onion, garlic, and herbs is known as *Ratatouille* (page 10) in France. It is a southern specialty, using olive oil to sauté the vegetables prior to braising them. Often made in large quantities, like any good stew, the leftovers are usually even tastier when reheated. One of the wonderful dishes to come out of ratatouille leftovers is pipérade, which is the stew reheated with eggs scrambled into it along with bacon or pancetta. This version is slightly different in that the leftovers are put in individual baking dishes, setting one or two eggs on top, and garnished with a dusting of Parmesan. Baked until golden, it is absolutely delicious, the Parmesan adding texture and salty notes to counterbalance an otherwise naturally sweet dish.

In individual baking or gratin dishes, add 1/2 cup ratatouille. Top with basil leaves, crack 1 or 2 eggs on top, and sprinkle with Parmesan cheese and pepper. Broil until golden and eggs are cooked to desired doneness, 3–5 minutes. Serve hot.

EXCHANGES / CHOICES
1 Vegetable
1 Protein, medium fat
1/2 Fat

Calories	130	
Calories from Fat	70	
Total Fat	8.0	g
Saturated Fat	2.1	g
Trans Fat	0.0	g
Cholesterol	185	mg
Sodium	75	mg
Potassium	280	mg
Total Carbohydrate	7	g
Dietary Fiber	2	g
Sugars	3	g
Protein	7	g
Phosphorus	125	mg

Quinoa with Kale and
Dried Cranberries (page 56)

Vegetable and Mushroom Frittata

SERVES 8

SERVING 1 wedge (1/2 cup)

PREP 15 minutes

COOK 15 minutes

PAIRING SUGGESTION
Curry Split Pea Soup (page 38) and Dates, Baby Arugula, and Stilton (page 106)

INGREDIENTS

3 tablespoons olive oil

1 medium onion, peeled and chopped

1 roasted orange bell pepper, stems and seeds removed, and chopped

1 pound brown cap mushrooms, stems trimmed, caps quartered

6 ounces baby spinach (about 5 cups)

4 large eggs, beaten

4 egg whites

Salt and pepper to taste

Frittata is a classic Spanish omelet that can be made ahead of time. And while the traditional frittata is made with onions and potatoes cooked in a generous amount of oil, you can use all sorts of vegetables to make a delicious version. Here I use spinach, mushrooms, and bell pepper, resulting in a light frittata that can be served with a salad on the side. Generally speaking, frittata is a great way to use up leftovers. Just chop whatever ingredient you have like roast chicken, or asparagus, or shrimp for variations on the theme. While frittata is usually flipped, here I broil it in the oven to finish it, avoiding any mess while giving you the same golden finish.

1 Preheat broiler, setting it on "low."

2 Meanwhile, in a small (8-inch) ovenproof skillet over medium heat, add 1 tablespoon oil and onions and bell peppers and cook until golden, about 5 minutes. Add the mushrooms and cook until soft, about 5 minutes. Transfer to a plate. Add 1 more tablespoon oil and sauté the spinach until wilted. Toss with the mushrooms mixture. Wipe the skillet clean and add the remaining oil, making sure to spread it evenly on the bottom and sides.

3 Pour 1/3 of the eggs and egg whites in and swirl to distribute evenly on bottom and sides. Scatter the sautéed vegetables all around and pour the remaining eggs and egg whites on top. Cook until the bottom is set and golden. Then place the skillet in the oven to finish, allowing the eggs to rise and become golden, 3–4 minutes. Remove from oven, slide onto a cutting board or plate, and slice. Leftovers are excellent as well.

EXCHANGES / CHOICES
1 Vegetable
1 Protein, lean
1 Fat

Calories	120
Calories from Fat	70
Total Fat	8.0 g
Saturated Fat	1.5 g
Trans Fat	0.0 g
Cholesterol	95 mg
Sodium	85 mg
Potassium	495 mg
Total Carbohydrate	6 g
Dietary Fiber	1 g
Sugars	2 g
Protein	7 g
Phosphorus	140 mg

Curry Split Pea Soup
(page 38)

Dates, Baby Arugula, and
Stilton (page 106)

Curry Shrimp with Peas

SERVES 8

SERVING 3/4 cup (2 oz shrimp)

PREP 10 minutes

COOK 10 minutes

PAIRING SUGGESTION
White Bean Salad with Golden Garlic Oil (page 68)

INGREDIENTS

3 tablespoons grapeseed oil

1 ounce ginger, peeled and paper-thinly sliced

5 large garlic cloves, crushed and peeled

1 pound small uncooked shrimp, peeled and deveined

1/2 teaspoon curry powder

1 cup fresh green peas

Salt and pepper to taste

Juice and grated zest of 1 lemon (about 1/4 cup)

Once of my favorite combination is shrimp with peas, infused with crispy ginger and garlic and spiced with a light dusting of curry powder. Have this colorful dish as is, served as an appetizer, or make it more substantial served over rice, Japanese buckwheat noodles, or angel hair pasta.

In a large skillet over high heat, add the oil and stir-fry the ginger and garlic until golden, about 3 minutes. Transfer to a plate, leaving the oil behind. Add the shrimp, curry, and lemon juice and stir-fry until cooked through and golden, about 5 minutes. Add the peas, season with salt and pepper, and stir-fry for 2–3 minutes more. Serve, garnished with stir-fried ginger and garlic and fresh lemon zest.

EXCHANGES / CHOICES
1/2 Carbohydrate
2 Protein, lean
1/2 Fat

Calories	125
Calories from Fat	55
Total Fat	6.0 g
Saturated Fat	0.7 g
Trans Fat	0.0 g
Cholesterol	90 mg
Sodium	485 mg
Potassium	190 mg
Total Carbohydrate	5 g
Dietary Fiber	1 g
Sugars	1 g
Protein	14 g
Phosphorus	150 mg

White Bean Salad with
Golden Garlic Oil (page 68)

Calamari in Tomato Sauce with Basil

SERVES 8

SERVING 1/2 cup (2 ounces squid)

PREP 15 minutes

COOK 25 minutes

PAIRING SUGGESTION

Black Bean and Red Bell Pepper Salad (page 58) and Avocado with Pink Grapefruit (page 104)

INGREDIENTS

2 tablespoons olive oil

4 large garlic cloves, crushed, peeled, and thinly sliced

1 large shallot, peeled and sliced into thin wedges

1 pound ripe sweet cherry tomatoes, halved

12 ounces fresh squid, cleaned and cut into rings

12 large basil leaves, freshly torn

Salt to taste

Red pepper flakes to taste

Squid, or "calamari," as it is often referred to, is delicious braised with tomatoes, garlic, fresh basil, and a touch of hot red pepper flakes. Simple and often served this way in Italy or France, it is delicious, colorful, and versatile. You can serve the dish as is with whole-grain bread on the side for scooping up the sauce, or you can also serve it over linguini or with steamed potatoes on the side. Don't forget to add a salad of fresh leafy greens or other vegetables and fruits for a balanced meal.

In a large skillet over medium heat, add the oil and sauté the garlic and shallots until golden, about 3 minutes. Add the tomatoes and 1 cup water. Cook until reduced and slightly thickened, about 15 minutes. Add the squid and continue to cook until cooked through, about 5 minutes. Toss in the basil and season with salt and red pepper flakes. Serve hot.

EXCHANGES / CHOICES
1 Vegetable
1 Protein, lean
1/2 Fat

Calories	90
Calories from Fat	35
Total Fat	4.0 g
Saturated Fat	0.7 g
Trans Fat	0.0 g
Cholesterol	115 mg
Sodium	25 mg
Potassium	250 mg
Total Carbohydrate	5 g
Dietary Fiber	1 g
Sugars	2 g
Protein	8 g
Phosphorus	105 mg

Black Bean and Red Bell
Pepper Salad (page 58)

Avocado with Pink
Grapefruit (page 104)

Broiled Miso
Salmon

SERVES 8

SERVING 6-ounce filet

PREP 48 hours

COOK 7 minutes

PAIRING SUGGESTION

Raw Zucchini Salad with Prunes (page 8) and Roasted Root Vegetables with Garlic (page 16)

INGREDIENTS

1/4 cup shiro-miso ("white" miso)

1/4 cup sake or light beer

1 tablespoon agave nectar

Four 6-ounce salmon filets

2 scallions, trimmed and thinly sliced diagonally

Miso-marinated fish has become a popular dish in fine establishments where black cod is often used. Any fish will do and will result in varied textures. You can marinate the fish for 1 hour, 12 hours, 24 hours, and up to 48 hours. The longer you marinate, the sweeter and more candied-like in appearance due to the fish undergoing a curing process. All sorts of white fish can be used, especially those with thick meaty flakes like cod. Salmon is also a great alternative and one of those fish that many seem to gravitate toward. Choose your favorite fish!

1 In a medium bowl, whisk together the miso, sake, and agave until smooth and well combined. Add the fish, coating each piece in the marinade until fully covered. Marinate for up to 48 hours, refrigerated.

2 Set the oven rack midway between the top and bottom of the oven and preheat the broiler. Drain and wipe the pieces of fish and place them on a baking sheet, an inch or so apart. Broil until caramelized and cooked through, but tender and ever so slightly translucent in the center, 5 to 7 minutes depending on thickness of each piece. Serve, garnished with scallions.

EXCHANGES / CHOICES
3 Protein, lean
1/2 Fat

Calories	165
Calories from Fat	70
Total Fat	8.0 g
Saturated Fat	1.3 g
Trans Fat	0.0 g
Cholesterol	60 mg
Sodium	130 mg
Potassium	275 mg
Total Carbohydrate	3 g
Dietary Fiber	0 g
Sugars	2 g
Protein	19 g
Phosphorus	200 mg

Raw Zucchini Salad with
Prunes (page 8)

Roasted Root Vegetables
with Garlic (page 16)

Pan-Seared Scallops with Avocado Walnut Sauce

SERVES 8

SERVING 3 scallops

PREP 15 minutes

COOK 5 minutes

PAIRING SUGGESTION

Butternut Squash Soup with Pine Nuts and Goji Berries (page 42) and Dates, Baby Arugula, and Stilton (page 106)

INGREDIENTS

1/2 cup cilantro, stems trimmed

Juice of 2 limes (about 1/3 cup)

2 ripe Hass avocados, halved, pitted, and peeled

1 jalapeño pepper, stem and seeds removed, chopped

1/3 cup raw walnuts

Salt and pepper to taste

2 tablespoons olive oil

24 large dry packed sea scallops, rinsed, drained, and patted dried

8 sprigs cilantro

Delicious, naturally sweet, and juicy, big sea scallops can be pan-seared to a golden crisp and served over a refreshing lime, cilantro, avocado, and walnut sauce. It can be a colorful appetizer or an entrée. You decide, but either way, your guests will be impressed by the flavors as much as by the textures and colors. You can even wrap the whole thing up in a fresh tortilla and pack it for lunch!

1 In a mini food processor, add the cilantro, lime juice, avocado, jalapeño, and walnuts. Process until smooth and divide equally among individual plates.

2 Meanwhile, season the scallops with salt and pepper. In a large skillet, add the oil and pan-fry the scallops until cooked through but slightly translucent in the center and golden crisp on the outside, about 3 minutes on the first side and 2 on the flip side. Drain on paper towels and arrange 3 scallops on each of the plates on top of the sauce. Garnish with a sprig of cilantro and serve hot.

EXCHANGES / CHOICES
1/2 Carbohydrate
1 Protein, lean
2 Fat

Basic Nutritional Values:

Calories	175
Calories from Fat	110
Total Fat	12.0 g
Saturated Fat	1.6 g
Trans Fat	0.0 g
Cholesterol	20 mg
Sodium	325 mg
Potassium	390 mg
Total Carbohydrate	8 g
Dietary Fiber	3 g
Sugars	1 g
Protein	11 g
Phosphorus	245 mg

Butternut Squash Soup with Pine Nuts and Goji Berries (page 42)

Dates, Baby Arugula, and Stilton (page 106)

Crab Cakes with Parsnip Purée

SERVES 8

SERVING 1 cake

PREP 20 minutes

COOK 25 minutes

PAIRING SUGGESTION

Roasted Brussels Sprouts and Butternut Squash (page 14) and Artichoke Hearts with Vinaigrette (page 20)

INGREDIENTS

- 6 parsnips, peeled and coarsely chopped
- 1 medium clove garlic, crushed and peeled
- 4 tablespoons olive oil, divided use
- 1 large shallot, peeled and minced
- 1 carrot, peeled and finely chopped
- 1 celery stick, finely chopped
- 2 pounds lump crabmeat (claw), drained
- 3 sprigs thyme, leaves only
- 1/2 teaspoon smoked paprika
- 2 large egg whites, beaten
- Salt and pepper to taste
- 1 cup oat bran
- 12 large fresh basil leaves, 6 julienned

I love a good crab cake, but more often than not, there's too much breading. Try these crab cakes for special occasions. Here the crab cake is mixed with caramelized onions, carrots, and celery and held together with a light dusting of oat bran. Pan-crisped, it is served atop a naturally sweet parsnip and basil purée. Note: you'll find lump crabmeat in specialty markets, the seafood counter, or in the frozen food section.

1. In a medium pot, add the parsnips and garlic with 2 cups water. Season with salt and pepper and cook until the vegetables are soft, about 15 minutes. Transfer to a blender with 2 cups of the cooking water and process until smooth. Set aside.

2. Meanwhile, in a skillet over medium heat, add 2 tablespoons oil and sauté the shallots, carrots, and celery until soft and golden, about 10 minutes.

3. In a large bowl, add the crabmeat, sautéed vegetables, thyme, smoked paprika, and egg whites. Season with salt and pepper and toss well. Divide into 8 equal portions and shape into round patties, about 3/4 inch thick. Sprinkle each cake with oat bran on all sides.

4. In a large skillet, add the remaining oil and cook the crab cakes until heated through and golden crisp, about 6 minutes, flipping once. Drain on paper towel.

5. To serve, spoon some parsnip sauce on individual plates and place one crab cake on top. Sprinkle with julienned basil leaves and serve.

EXCHANGES / CHOICES
1 Starch
3 Protein, lean
1/2 Fat

Calories	240
Calories from Fat	80
Total Fat	9.0 g
Saturated Fat	1.3 g
Trans Fat	0.0 g
Cholesterol	95 mg
Sodium	300 mg
Potassium	700 mg
Total Carbohydrate	19 g
Dietary Fiber	4 g
Sugars	4 g
Protein	23 g
Phosphorus	305 mg

Roasted Brussels Sprouts and Butternut Squash (page 14)

Artichoke Hearts with Vinaigrette (page 20)

Ginger Lobster Salad

SERVES 8

SERVING 1 cup

PREP 20 minutes

COOK 0 minutes

PAIRING SUGGESTION

Raw Zucchini Salad with Prunes (page 8) and Spicy Lemon-Sesame Hummus (page 66)

Lobsters are often associated with that occasional special celebratory meal. They are costly, but once in a while when you feel like splurging, try this delicious lobster salad. This one is healthy, minus the thick, rich mayonnaise sauce often associated with it. A touch of olive oil, some grated ginger with at drizzle of tamari makes this lobster salad light with unexpected flavors. Perfect served over rice and stir-fried greens on the side.

INGREDIENTS

- 2 pounds cooked lobster meat only, chopped
- 1 celery stalk, quartered lengthwise and finely sliced
- 1/4 orange bell pepper, stem and seeds removed, finely diced
- 1/2 ounce ginger, peeled and grated (about 1 1/2 teaspoons)
- 1 teaspoon lower-sodium soy
- 1 tablespoon rice vinegar (regular, unseasoned)
- 1 teaspoon dark sesame oil
- 1 teaspoon grapeseed oil
- 1/2 teaspoon sriracha or other hot sauce
- 8 sprigs cilantro, leaves only

In a medium bowl, add the lobster, celery, bell pepper, ginger, soy, vinegar, sesame and grapeseed oils, and sriracha. Toss well and garnish each serving with some cilantro.

You can buy pre-boiled lobsters or simply cook them yourself. If you choose the latter option, make sure you bring a large pot of water to a boil and add the lobsters, head in first to kill them instantly. No sense in making them suffer! Once cooked, remove all meat to use in the recipe, and reserve the shells and heads for making stock and lobster bisque, for example.

EXCHANGES / CHOICES
3 Protein, lean

Calories	125
Calories from Fat	20
Total Fat	2.0 g
Saturated Fat	0.3 g
Trans Fat	0.0 g
Cholesterol	80 mg
Sodium	465 mg
Potassium	445 mg
Total Carbohydrate	2 g
Dietary Fiber	0 g
Sugars	0 g
Protein	24 g
Phosphorus	215 mg

Raw Zucchini Salad with
Prunes (page 8)

Spicy Lemon-Sesame
Hummus (page 66)

Curry-Spiced Chicken Breasts

SERVES 8

SERVING 4 oz chicken

PREP 10 minutes

COOK 10 minutes

PAIRING SUGGESTIONS
Smoked Tomato Bean Soup
(page 40) and Quinoa with Kale
and Dried Cranberries (page 56)

INGREDIENTS
3 tablespoons olive oil
1 tablespoon curry powder
1 tablespoon grated garlic
1 tablespoon grated ginger
Salt and pepper to taste
2 pounds boneless and skinless
      chicken breast (4 halves)

One of the easiest things to cook is chicken. A versatile protein, it's the "go-to" for many home cooks. For many, it spells "comfort" whether cooked plain, spiced, or marinated. And the leftovers can be chopped and used for stir-fries as is common in Asian cuisines, or sliced and added to wraps. This recipe is a great way to make use of curry powder, here further enhanced with garlic and ginger.

1 Preheat the broiler to "High" for 20 minutes, placing the rack midway in the center of the oven.

2 In a mixing bowl, stir together the olive oil, curry, garlic, and ginger. Season with salt and pepper. Add the chicken and toss until every piece is coated evenly through-out. Place the chicken breasts on a baking sheet and broil until the juices run clear and the top is golden, about 10 minutes. Let rest for 15 minutes before slicing.

EXCHANGES / CHOICES
4 Protein, lean

Calories	175
Calories from Fat	70
Total Fat	8.0 g
Saturated Fat	1.5 g
Trans Fat	0.0 g
Cholesterol	65 mg
Sodium	60 mg
Potassium	220 mg
Total Carbohydrate	1 g
Dietary Fiber	0 g
Sugars	0 g
Protein	24 g
Phosphorus	180 mg

Smoked Tomato Bean Soup (page 40)

Quinoa with Kale and Dried Cranberries (page 56)

Rosemary-Sage Turkey Breast

SERVES 8

SERVING 4 ounces turkey

PREP 10 minutes

COOK 30 minutes

PAIRING SUGGESTION
Butternut Squash Soup with Pine Nuts and Goji Berries (page 42) and Ratatouille (page 10)

INGREDIENTS

3 tablespoons rosemary leaves (about 3 sprigs)

1/3 cup sage leaves (about 4 sprigs)

1 garlic head or 8 cloves, peeled

1 lemon, peeled and sectioned

3 tablespoons olive oil

Salt and pepper to taste

2 pounds boneless and skinless turkey breast (one half)

This rosemary and garlic herbal paste is delicious on meat, poultry, and seafood, especially swordfish, tuna, or salmon. It's also a great herb paste for flavoring rice or roast potatoes. Leftover turkey breast is also great to have. Sliced cold, you can add it to salads or wraps. You can also make turkey vegetable soup or turkey chili on a cold winter day.

1 Preheat the oven to 400°F for 20 minutes.

2 Meanwhile, in a small food processor, add the rosemary and sage leaves, garlic, lemon, olive oil, and salt and pepper. Process to a paste consistency. Poke holes in the turkey breast (rounded side up), every inch or so, driving the thick side of a chopstick almost all the way through but not quite. Fill each hole with paste, rubbing the leftover all over the top and bottom of the breast. Place the turkey breast on a baking sheet and roast until the juices run just about clear, about 25 to 30 minutes. Turn on the broiler on high and cook until golden crisp, 3 to 5 minutes more. Let rest for 15 minutes before carving.

EXCHANGES / CHOICES
4 Protein, lean

Calories	175
Calories from Fat	55
Total Fat	6.0 g
Saturated Fat	0.9 g
Trans Fat	0.0 g
Cholesterol	75 mg
Sodium	50 mg
Potassium	295 mg
Total Carbohydrate	2 g
Dietary Fiber	0 g
Sugars	0 g
Protein	27 g
Phosphorus	210 mg

Butternut Squash Soup with Pine Nuts and Goji Berries (page 42)

Ratatouille (page 10)

Pan-Seared Pork Tenderloin with Sautéed Apples

SERVES 8

SERVING 4 ounces pork

PREP 20 minutes

COOK 15 minutes

PAIRING SUGGESTION
Oak Leaf Lettuce and Pear Salad with Stilton (page 4) and Roasted Root Vegetables with Garlic (page 16)

INGREDIENTS
1/4 cup olive oil plus
  2 tablespoons more if
  necessary, divided use
4 Granny Smith apples, cored
  and sliced into 1/4-inch-thick
  wedges
1 large yellow onion, peeled
  and sliced into 1/4-inch-thick
  wedges
24 fresh medium to large basil
  leaves, torn
2 pounds pork tenderloin, cut
  into 1-inch-thick medallions
Salt and pepper to taste

Sautéed apples and fruit in general are great accompaniments to pork dishes. The meat lends itself well to fruit relishes. Here I use Granny Smith apples. Sliced in thick wedges, they are tender yet crispy at the same time for a balanced texture. The pork tenderloin, cut in 1-inch-thick medallions, is pan-seared until crispy on the outside and medium to medium well on the inside, depending on desired doneness. Serve with a salad for a healthy meal.

1 In a large skillet over medium heat, add 2 tablespoons olive oil and sauté the apples and onions until golden, softer yet still firm, about 10 minutes. Season with salt and pepper, add the basil, toss, and transfer to a serving dish or divide among individual plates.

2 Meanwhile in another skillet over medium heat, add the remaining oil. Season the pork medallions with salt and pepper on both sides and sear the pieces until golden crisp on both side and tender and juicy on the inside, about 4 minutes total, flipping once. Place the pork medallions on top of the apples and serve hot.

EXCHANGES / CHOICES
1/2 Fruit
1 Vegetable
3 Protein, lean
1/2 Fat

Calories	230
Calories from Fat	90
Total Fat	10.0 g
Saturated Fat	2.0 g
Trans Fat	0.0 g
Cholesterol	60 mg
Sodium	40 mg
Potassium	480 mg
Total Carbohydrate	13 g
Dietary Fiber	2 g
Sugars	9 g
Protein	22 g
Phosphorus	215 mg

Oak Leaf Lettuce and
Pear Salad with Stilton
(page 4)

Roasted Root Vegetables
with Garlic (page 16)

Pork Lettuce Wrap with Prune Relish

SERVES 8

SERVES 8

SERVING 3 ounces pork

PREP 10 minutes

COOK 10 minutes

PAIRING SUGGESTION

Spicy Miso Guacamole
(page 22) and Tabbouleh with
Cucumber and Tomatoes
(page 54)

INGREDIENTS

2 tablespoons olive oil

1 small onion, peeled and
   minced

2 large garlic cloves, peeled and
   minced

10 pitted prunes, minced

1 sprig rosemary, leaves only,
   minced

Salt and pepper to taste

1 1/2 pounds pork tenderloin,
   sliced into thin strips

1 head tender lettuce such as
   Bibb, Boston, or oak leaf

3 scallions, trimmed and thinly
   sliced diagonally

Lettuce wraps are a fun way to eat all sorts of braised or sautéed meat, seafood, or vegetarian dishes. Here tender and lean pork tenderloin strips are cooked in a sweet and savory prune, onion, and rosemary relish, then wrapped in lettuce for a balanced, refreshing, and relatively light meal. So simple to make, you'll have a meal on the table in less than 20 minutes.

In a large skillet over medium heat, add the oil, onion, garlic, prunes, rosemary, and 1/3 cup water. Season with salt and pepper and cook until reduced to a paste consistency, about 5 minutes. Add the pork and continue to sauté until the meat is cooked through and well coated, another 5 minutes. To eat, take a lettuce leaf, add some pork with prune relish, and garnish with scallions.

EXCHANGES / CHOICES
1/2 Carbohydrate
2 Protein, lean
1/2 Fat

Calories	155
Calories from Fat	55
Total Fat	6.0 g
Saturated Fat	1.2 g
Trans Fat	0.0 g
Cholesterol	45 mg
Sodium	35 mg
Potassium	425 mg
Total Carbohydrate	9 g
Dietary Fiber	1 g
Sugars	5 g
Protein	17 g
Phosphorus	170 mg

Spicy Miso Guacamole
(page 22)

Tabbouleh with Cucumber
and Tomatoes (page 54)

FRUIT, CHEESE, NUTS, & SEEDS

Desserts or sweet snacks should be considered "sometimes foods." The occasional bite will often soothe the soul. Think of desserts as a treat and taste, two or three bites is often plenty to satisfy that sweet tooth. The focus in this chapter is fruit, cheese, nuts, and seeds, a perfect combination of naturally earthy and sweet flavors, with soft and crunchy textures. A perfect way to end the meal!

If we look at different food cultures, we notice that these types of foods are often had as an afternoon pick-me-up with either tea or coffee. In this same vein, perhaps reserve these recipes for the weekend or holidays, when gathering with family and friends to share in the good times. Think slivers, or light, delicate, and sensible bites as your goal when approaching the next few recipes.

I've cut back significantly on sugars and fats, relying instead on the natural sweetness and richness of the main ingredients.

Berries with Balsamic and Fresh Basil

SERVES 8

SERVING 1/2 cup

PREP 15 minutes

COOK 0 minutes

PAIRING SUGGESTIONS
End any meal with fresh fruit

INGREDIENTS

1 cup blackberries

1 cup raspberries

1 cup blueberries

12 strawberries

3 tablespoons good quality aged balsamic

Olive oil for light drizzling (optional)

1/3 cup small basil leaves, or 12 large freshly torn ones

A take on the popular Mediterranean strawberries soaked in balsamic, or red wine as is the case with the French, here I combine all sorts of berries in season. Drizzled with sweet, tangy, aged balsamic with freshly torn basil, this dessert is perfect on a hot summer day. Eat it for breakfast, as an appetizer, afternoon snack, or dessert. This is one of those dishes that won't put you over the edge after a meal but might instead help with digestion, while refreshing the palate.

Toss the berries with balsamic and divide among individual servings, each drizzled lightly with olive oil, if using, and garnished with basil.

EXCHANGES / CHOICES
1/2 Fruit

Calories	35	
Calories from Fat	0	
Total Fat	0.0	g
Saturated Fat	0.0	g
Trans Fat	0.0	g
Cholesterol	0	mg
Sodium	0	mg
Potassium	110	mg
Total Carbohydrate	9	g
Dietary Fiber	3	g
Sugars	5	g
Protein	1	g
Phosphorus	15	mg

Apple Cranberry Pecan Crisp

SERVES 12

SERVING 1/2 cup

PREP 20 minutes

COOK 50 minutes

INGREDIENTS

8 large Granny Smith apples, peeled, cored, and chopped

12 ounces fresh cranberries

3/4 cup sugar, divided use

2 1/2 cups rolled oats

1/2 cup whole-wheat flour

1 cup crushed raw or roasted unsalted walnuts

4 tablespoons canola oil

2 tablespoons vanilla extract

Autumn's colorful and glorious foliage comes around and I think crisp with one of the most delicious combinations, apple, cranberry, and walnuts. On the tart side with not too much sugar added, this crisp relies on the natural flavors of the fruit. One of the easiest desserts to make, it is also a perfect breakfast, including fruit, nuts, and rolled oats.

Preheat the oven to 375°F for 20 minutes. In a large rectangular baking dish (9 × 12-inch), add the apples, cranberries, and half the sugar and toss well. In a medium bowl, add the rolled oats, flour, remaining sugar, walnuts, canola oil, and vanilla extract. Mix well and scatter over the apples and cranberries. Bake until the apples are soft, the juices surface, and the topping is golden, about 50 minutes, covering midway with aluminum foil, if necessary.

EXCHANGES / CHOICES
3 1/2 Carbohydrate
2 Fat

Calories	315	
Calories from Fat	110	
Total Fat	12.0	g
Saturated Fat	1.1	g
Trans Fat	0.0	g
Cholesterol	0	mg
Sodium	0	mg
Potassium	280	mg
Total Carbohydrate	51	g
Dietary Fiber	6	g
Sugars	29	g
Protein	5	g
Phosphorus	135	mg

Banana, Blueberry, and Pecan Shake

SERVES 8

SERVING 8 ounces

PREP 5 minutes

COOK 0 minutes

INGREDIENTS

1 ripe banana, peeled

1/2 cup blueberries

1/3 cup raw pecans

1 tablespoon flaxseed meal

1 quart unsweetened pure
coconut water

The healthiest, most nutritious protein shake is made at home with wholesome ingredients and nothing else. Here is a quick and delicious energy booster, loaded with vitamins and minerals. Perfect for breakfast or as an afternoon snack.

In a blender, add the banana, berries, pecans, flaxseed meal, and coconut water. Process until smooth.

Start with a banana, which gives the shake its smooth texture, and then use 1/2 cup of any other fresh fruit or berry to make this shake.

EXCHANGES / CHOICES
1 Carbohydrate
1/2 Fat

Calories	75
Calories from Fat	35
Total Fat	4.0 g
Saturated Fat	0.3 g
Trans Fat	0.0 g
Cholesterol	0 mg
Sodium	30 mg
Potassium	295 mg
Total Carbohydrate	11 g
Dietary Fiber	2 g
Sugars	7 g
Protein	1 g
Phosphorus	35 mg

Avocado with Pink Grapefruit

SERVES 8

SERVING 1 cup

PREP 10 minutes

COOK 0 minutes

INGREDIENTS

3 ripe Hass avocados, halved, pitted, peeled, and cut into bite-size pieces

1 large pink grapefruit, peeled, membrane removed from each section, pieces halved

4 sprigs cilantro, leaves only

Salt and pepper to taste

Avocados are high in protein and one of the best foods you can eat. They help reduce bad cholesterol while increasing metabolism. Mixed with refreshing pink grapefruit, this nutrient-rich fruit salad is perfect any time of the day as a full meal, appetizer, or snack. In small doses, the acidity of the grapefruit complements the richness of avocado well. A touch of salt and pepper and a few cilantro leaves, and you can enjoy this simple salad for breakfast, lunch, or dinner.

In a medium bowl, gently toss the avocado and grapefruit pieces, and garnish with cilantro. Serve, lightly seasoned with salt and pepper.

EXCHANGES / CHOICES
1/2 Fruit
2 Fat

Calories	110	
Calories from Fat	80	
Total Fat	9.0	g
Saturated Fat	1.2	g
Trans Fat	0.0	g
Cholesterol	0	mg
Sodium	5	mg
Potassium	360	mg
Total Carbohydrate	8	g
Dietary Fiber	4	g
Sugars	3	g
Protein	1	g
Phosphorus	35	mg

Dates, Baby Arugula, and Stilton

SERVES 8

SERVING 2 pieces

PREP 15 minutes

COOK 0 minutes

INGREDIENTS

16 fresh Medjool dates, split
lengthwise, halfway through
to remove pit

16 baby arugula leaves

1/3 cup crumbled Stilton or
other blue cheese

One of my favorite fruits on the planet is the date. When they're at the market, I load up. I love their naturally sweet taste and soft, gooey texture. When paired with baby arugula and Stilton—arguably the king of blue cheeses—the results are sublime and perfect for bringing to a summer picnic at the park.

On a serving platter, arrange the dates, cut side up, about 1 inch apart. Add 1 arugula leaf on top of each, and top with about 1/2 teaspoon cheese.

EXCHANGES / CHOICES
2 1/2 Fruit

Calories	155
Calories from Fat	15
Total Fat	1.5 g
Saturated Fat	1.0 g
Trans Fat	0.1 g
Cholesterol	5 mg
Sodium	80 mg
Potassium	360 mg
Total Carbohydrate	36 g
Dietary Fiber	3 g
Sugars	32 g
Protein	2 g
Phosphorus	55 mg

Baked Goat Cheese
with Bosc Pear

SERVES 8

SERVING 1 tablespoon
goat cheese. plus
3 pear wedges

PREP 15 minutes

COOK O minutes

INGREDIENTS

1 (4-ounce) log fresh goat
    cheese, "low-salt"

2 teaspoons olive oil

1/2 teaspoon curry powder

1 teaspoon fennel seeds

2 teaspoons raw sunflower
    seeds

1 tablespoon raw pumpkin
    seeds

1 sprig fresh thyme, leaves only

2 ripe Bosc pears, halved, cored,
    and sliced into 1/8-inch thin
    wedges lengthwise

Cheese is delicious and a little will go a long way. This baked goat cheese dusted lightly with curry and garnished with seeds and herbs is absolutely delicious scooped up with sweet, ripe, juicy slices of Bosc pears. This recipe will quickly become a favorite with your friends and family. Feel free to experiment with all sorts of nuts, seeds, and every dried fruit, if you so desire. Serve with toast points, crackers, but I must admit that pears are the perfect complement to this creamy, ever so slightly tangy goat cheese.

1 Preheat the oven to 400°F for 20 minutes.

2 In the center of a baking or gratin dish, place the goat cheese log. Drizzle with olive oil and sprinkle with curry powder. Scatter the fennel, sunflower, and pumpkin seeds. Garnish with thyme leaves and bake until soft and lightly golden, about 15 minutes. Serve hot with sliced pears.

EXCHANGES / CHOICES

1/2 Fruit

1 Fat

Calories	75	
Calories from Fat	30	
Total Fat	3.5	g
Saturated Fat	1.0	g
Trans Fat	0.0	g
Cholesterol	0	mg
Sodium	50	mg
Potassium	80	mg
Total Carbohydrate	8	g
Dietary Fiber	2	g
Sugars	5	g
Protein	3	g
Phosphorus	60	mg

INDEX